to Rita
the 1.

D1500170

Edith Rylander

RURAL ROUTES

Rural Routes

Essays on Living in Rural Minnesota

Edith Rylander

NORTH STAR PRESS OF ST. CLOUD, INC.

This book is for
my mother,
Ellen Alcock Tarver,
and, in loving memory, for
Elsie Rylander Larson

Library of Congress Cataloging-in-Publication Data
Rylander, Edith.
    Rural routes : essays on living in rural Minnesota / Edith
Rylander.
        128 p. 21½ cm.
        ISBN 0-87839-079-0 : $9.95
        1. Country life—Minnesota.   2. Minnesota—Social life and
customs.   I. Title.
F610.R95   1993
977.6'00973'4--dc20   93-4854
                                                                                                               CIP

Cover photo by Myron Hall, used with permission of the Stearns
County Historical Society.

Printed in the United States of America by Versa Press, Inc., East
Peoria, Illinois.

Published by North Star Press of St. Cloud, Inc., P.O. Box 451,
St. Cloud, Minnesota 56302.

ISBN: 0-87839-079-0

Author's Note

My first newspaper column appeared in the *Long Prairie Leader* on March 5, 1980. I had been writing poetry since childhood and fiction since I was a teenager, but I never would have started writing newspaper columns without the firm, unrelenting pressure of my domestic partner, John. And I never would have gotten into the week-in, week-out routine of column writing if Sherry Breen, then editing the *Leader*, hadn't given me a chance at biweekly appearances in its pages.

Another friend, Claire Peske, brought my column, "Rural Routes," to the attention of editor Bob Wright at the *Morrison County Record*. The column has been appearing weekly in the *Record* since May 26, 1980. And a monthly, untitled column of mine has run in the *St. Cloud Daily Times* since Independence Day 1983.

Living in a part of the world where people still wave when they pass me on the road, to write a newspaper column is to have my ideas, observations, and, to some extent, my life events become part of public dialogue. "I was sorry to read that you lost your cat," says a lady, whom I don't remember having met, at the garden store. I realize that by writing about Sam, I made him everyone's cat in a sense. I am a private person, and Sam was a private cat; all this takes a little getting used to.

It's my personal conviction that all of us, even if we don't live on rural routes, have more in common than we think. We all live on the same earth. We all love people. We all want our families to thrive and survive us.

I've tried in these columns to reach out to that common ground of life experience through my own life here in the southeast corner of Todd County, Minnesota, to share with others the funny, gritty, touching and puzzling business of being a woman, a mother, a gardener and stock raiser, an American, and a citizen of the third planet from the sun.

I'm grateful to the *Long Prairie Leader*, the *Morrison County Record*, and the *St. Cloud Daily Times*, in which these columns first appeared, for giving me space and freedom in which to explore that common ground.

Edith Rylander

Contents

Work

Seasons

Family

Nature

Work

There was a time in my childhood when, while putting off setting the table or mowing the lawn so slowly that I could have grown moss, I used to have dreamy fantasies of machines that would do all my work for me, leaving me free to read, write and experience life, which I thought more appropriate for a "literary person." Probably it's just as well that those fantasies were not fulfilled.

Lambing

March 5, 1984

Just before lambing, the ewes spend a lot of time lying around breathing heavily. They look like great bags of beige-grey wool, improbably equipped with slim dark legs and melancholy, patient faces. Now and then the wool ripples or jerks as the unborn lambs kick inside.

We have reached the time of year when it isn't sufficient to check the livestock morning and evening. It's 3:00 a.m., and I'm going out to check the ewes. Under winter stars I pick my way across the yard in thick, waffle-soled boots, crossing the icy patch by the end of the garage with caution, breaking through surface frost and sliding in greasy mud as I cross the driveway between the cattle shed and the pole barn.

I switch on the flashlight and count the sheep outside the corral. Ten, that's right. None in labor, so far as I can see. That leaves the two in the barn, the two we penned up because they'd been bred first.

As I open the door I can hear a hoarse, panting sound. I switch on the light. It's Granny, a big grey-nosed ewe in the second pen.

For a moment as she swings around, I am seeing something monstrous. Granny is half squatting. In the cold night her nostrils jet steam. She's breathing harshly, making a pounding sound like

3

a steam engine. Her muzzle is covered with froth and her teeth show. Below her pushing haunches, lurching as she strains to be delivered, is a slimy, dark lump.

I take one step closer, and the lump is a head—the head of a lamb still in its birth membrane, which puffs faintly in and out over the nostrils. I can see both ears. And a foot. One foot.

Lambs normally exit the intra-uterine world in the attitude of a diver, front feet under chin. I climb into the pen with Granny and pull the wool aside so I can see better. She flinches away, but I'm sure now. There's only one foot out, which means the other front leg is hung up inside.

I've read through the section on deliveries in the book, the one with the line drawings, one leg back, both legs back, hind legs presenting, back presenting, twins tangled together. I also have vivid memories of the ewe two years back that we found in this situation. I had read all the instructions in the book—how you reach in, how you move things around. But when I tried it that time the lamb wound up dead. It was nearly dead when we got there, and it was an enormous lamb. But it was my first try, and it failed.

I stand back. Granny is pushing with all her strength. I've never seen an animal work like that. The head, breath faintly stirring the membrane, is still just where it was. Go in the house and wake up my husband? He could get her down and on her back, "cast" her, as they call it in the sheep book. It might make a delivery easier. But he's more tired than I am, he wakes up more easily and more often.

Granny heaves again. When she does that, my abdominal muscles and lower back muscles tighten sympathetically. If this goes on much longer we may lose both ewe and lamb.

I step toward her, pretending a confidence I don't feel. She stands when I touch her. I take a deep breath and slide my hand in.

The hot, slick inside of this different body clasps my hand with alien muscles. What I feel doesn't seem to have much to do with those line drawings in the book, or with words. But this is neck, and what's this, shoulder? Pushing against the pelvic girdle? If I can just change the angle a little.

There's a little shifting, Granny's muscles are pushing down. I yank my hand away, and now there are two legs out. Then a heave, and a lamb out to the hips. Then one more heave and the whole dark, glistening bag full of lamb is squirming on the straw.

I think about breaking the birth sack, stripping the membrane, but Granny is licking the lamb off, tearing and eating away membrane. The lamb bleats. She answers, less a bleat than a reassuring mutter, cleaning forward along the body. The membrane comes away from the face.

Before all the membrane is off, the little black ewe lamb is up on its knees, bleating like anything. Three-fourths of the way through the cleaning job, Granny delivers another lamb. I stand at the fence and watch, though there's nothing left for me to do, as Granny cleans and nuzzles and the lambs bleat and stagger around and look for milk. Two healthy little ewes.

I find I'm dozing against the fence. I stump back to the house, wash my hands well, throw off my clothes, fall into bed. It's 4:20, and we have eleven ewes to go.

ST. CLOUD TIMES

Planting Out

May 2, 1983

"If you want to get out there with those kohlrabies," John said as he dressed for work, "you'd better hurry. It's rumbling out in the west."

Rumbling it was and looking mighty purple. The rain we had been looking for these last dry, windy days, the rain to start off our newly-planted onions, peas, parsnips, radishes, and carrots, might be out in those burgeoning clouds.

The ideal conditions for transplanting are a combination of calm, mildness, and overcast. I carried out the flat of kohlrabies that we had started in the basement greenhouse. I also brought up some garlic heads, mine from last fall, and a can full of assorted seed packets—beets and broccoli and lettuce. Cautiously, I left the seed packets in the entryway. No point in getting them wet if it did rain.

Out in the garden I skipped the usual moment of meditative pleasure in which I stand and admire our good crumbly soil, so much easier to work than when we started gardening in this spot ten springs ago. During those ten years, load after load of compost, manure, and animal bedding has been dug into the soil. We haven't yet attained the kind of soil found when leaf mold is scratched away in the deep woods—peaty black soil that crumbles in the fingers. But we keep working at it. Ten years ago the soil in the top end of our garden, even after plowing and cultivating, had the consistency of broken brick. Now it's good friable soil. We're proud of that.

However, this morning I skipped admiring our soil. The rumbling John had mentioned was getting closer. Indeed, as I set down my flat of kohlrabi plants by the garden, I saw a flash of lightning off to the northwest. From the distant, diffuse rumblings, I judged that it was still several miles away. I'd keep an eye on it. But there was work to be done.

Only another gardener probably understands the full urgency of getting things out in the spring. After the long snowy time, when all gardening takes place on window sills, comes that period of early spring that seems to go on forever. Skies are gloomy, temperatures are above freezing but chilly, last year's grass has an ash-and-bone color. Started things get leggy in their flats. The seed packet pictures of lush growth look like maddening hallucinations. Then all of a sudden it's real spring, planting time; the soil is workable, the temperature warm enough to move around outside without being wrapped like a mummy. And everything needs to go into the ground at once.

Dark sky or not, it was a pleasant morning. All the newly-returned birds were singing: robins, red-winged blackbirds down in the swamp, song sparrows, the first white-throated sparrow of the season calling out "Old Sam Peabody, Peabody, Peabody," the first loons I've heard chattering out on Swan Lake, and whatever kind of bird it is that goes "Wicky, Wicky, Wicky." I didn't want to drop my planting and go get the field glasses and bird book to identify the "wicky" bird.

I used my hoe-handle row spacer and stakes and string to lay out a row next to the one I had planted the last time I was out there. I have to be careful laying out rows, for some deviousness in my character always brings them out curved. This makes life interesting for John or Eric when they come through with the garden tiller. If all the curves ran the same way it wouldn't be so bad, but they bow in and out, so that it looks as if I am trying to execute Dolly Parton's silhouette in string beans.

Row lined out, I grabbed the small shovel and charged down the line, digging little holes about ten inches apart. More lightning, a little closer, but nary a spit of rain. Down the row with a bucket of water, filling each hole. Then the tricky part: using the old, dull knife blade to separate a cluster of tiny kohlrabi plants from each other. Planted, once past the droopy stage of transplant trauma, they would grow big and vigorous, their bulbous, crispy, white stems adorning our snack plates and salad bowls. Then the most delicate part of all: lifting the plant by its leaves, tucking its hair-like roots down into the wet earth, scraping in other earth to fill.

First row done. But there were still plenty of plants in the flat. Well, the lightning wasn't that close. Measure with row spacer, drive in stakes, grab up shovel, dig holes, pour water in holes, separate plants, tuck plants into damp dirt, done!

And still not a drop of rain, though on the far side of the lake the undersides of clouds had that fringy look. But still, maybe I could get the last of the garlic in. Make the little holes, quickly, quickly. (The thunder was making very interesting noises then, like a 747 heard at a distance or a roller-skating rink.) Drop in the little cloves, blunt side down, sharp side up, one to a hole. (First drops of rain began to patter down.) Scrape dirt over the garlic buds to cover. Suddenly real rain bounced on my back. Bouncing hard. Stinging. Rice-size hail pelting me as I threw on the last dirt, laid the shovel down across the bed to mark where I finished, and ran for it. I didn't pack down the dirt over the garlic planting, I thought as I ran up the path to the house. But the rain will do it for me.

Postscript: Alas, thunder, hail, and all, we didn't get more than an eighth of an inch of rain out of that shower and are back waiting.

MORRISON COUNTY RECORD

Sheepshearing

May 9, 1983

The sheep-shearers were over this afternoon.

Everybody knows that the wool which goes into cloth, sweaters, and fine carpeting starts out on the back of sheep, but not too many people have actually seen the shearing operation. Like a lot of agricultural tasks, clipping the wool off sheep sounds simple in theory but gets complicated in practice.

To begin with, sheep may be panting in their coats of shaggy grey wool, but that doesn't mean that they will stroll up to the shearer like women going in for beauty-parlor appointments. The same sheep that will follow us around the pen if they think we have some grain, or just out of sociability and curiosity, will bolt and run if we try to corner them.

Since the shearers had come to shear sheep and not to corral them, we first separated out our bull calves, Star and Roscoe. Then we penned the ewes in the barn away from their lambs, who of course began bleating piteously.

About the time we finished this job the shearers drove up. They rigged the hanging frames to which their powered shears were attached and laid out the big sheets of plywood on which the shearing takes place. Then they were ready for their first customers. Eric and John grabbed one ewe from the flock, which was milling and blatting in the corner of the pen. As they aimed her out the door, I slammed the gate behind her. She was squirming and struggling and thrashing around. I would not have thought anybody could separate her from her fleece without bloodshed on the part of either sheep or shearer.

The first thing a shearer does is take the sheep down. Our book on sheep care has a section called "Shearing in Twenty Steps," which begins, "Slip left thumb into sheep's mouth, back of the incisor teeth. . . ." Better the shearer than me! But once the sheep is off her feet and realizes she can't escape, she relaxes philosophically and becomes perfectly still. For a good part of the shearing process she is sitting up on her rump, her mild face gazing patiently into the middle distance, and her slim front legs hanging down over her belly.

A competent shearer takes the fleece off in long, easy strokes, so that it comes away in one piece. The outer fleece is always more or less grey with dirt and grime, but as it peals away we see the creamy white inner fleece which has been spun, woven, knitted, and prized since the Bronze Age. We also see the bare body of the nursing ewes emerging from that great ball of fluff in which they have looked like wooly blobs with heads and legs. By the time they were finished being shorn, our sheep had shrunk by about one-third.

Each fleece was rolled together, with odd tags and exceptionally dirty chunks discarded. Then it was weighed and put into the giant wool sack.

As each slenderized ewe was liberated, she ran off to join the others. It was quite clear, from all the sniffing and milling and head bumping going on, that, without thir wool, the sheep looked as strange to each other as they did to us. Sheep have a butting order, as chickens have a pecking order. A new ewe coming into the herd has to find her place in relation to the others through establishing who butts whom. Our ewes are very gentle with people and have never given me so much as a bump, but they will crack each other head-on. Our shorn ewes were behaving exactly as if they had just met. All over the pen, heads were thumping.

The lambs very quickly figured out who their mothers were and were nursing within minutes—nursing more visibly than when the wool had hung down, completely obscuring the udder. Often it's hard to tell in the first day or two after birth whether a lamb is nursing or not, and the conscientious shepherd will often wind up on his or her knees in cold dirty straw, groping underneath a skittish ewe to establish by touch if the little lamb has gotten a good grip on the life-giving spigot.

My ideas about animal nursing, coming as I do from a sub-urban background, had largely been formed by movies like *My Friend Flicka*. In other words, spotless mares in spotless stalls nursing spotless foals, with none of the anatomical detail very clear. When a lamb nurses, especially the first few times, it is every bit as touching as when an animal nurses in a Disney studios movie, but it is a bit rougher. For one thing, sheep are built too low to the ground for lambs to nurse standing. They nurse on their front knees, behinds hoisted and heads twisted back at an angle that would be extremely uncomfortable for a human. (The lambs don't seem to mind, though.) Once having assumed nursing position, the lamb makes it emphatically clear to the ewe that it is hungry by butting her in the udder, and I mean really butting—hard. This is said to stimulate milk production, though if the watching shep-herd has done any breast-feeding she is likely to wince sympa-thetically as she watches. A lamb even a few days old can butt hard enough to jar its mother, and when twins nurse simultaneously it's not uncommon to see the poor old lady's south end hoisted right off the ground by the combined hunger of her offspring.

By suppertime our wool was on its way to market, and our sheep were grazing peaceably. Every once in a while, one of our svelte and woolless ewes would give a little caper, enjoying her new lightness.

MORRISON COUNTY RECORD

Planting

May 14, 1981

These days there is always dirt on the knees of my pants and under my fingernails, and there are always seed packets in my pockets. As I fall asleep, my fingers remember the feel of damp or gritty earth, my back remembers alterations of warmth or cold as clouds cross the sun, my eyes under closed eyelids still keep the shapes of corn grains or round brown radish seeds or almost invisible seeds of carrot and lettuce. It's planting season.

Some people shake their heads over "all that work, when you could go down to the store and buy it." It is true that, by growing all our vegetables and most of our meat, John and I save a certain amount of money. But people who dislike getting dirt under their nails will never be sweet-talked into gardening by the promise of saving money. Planting things and watching them grow is subject to all the joys and frustrations of parenting.

Now and again in the paper I see a list of all the expenses involved in raising a child. So much for medical care, so much for clothing, so much for education. It runs up into the thousands of dollars. Is anybody who really wants a child deterred from parenthood by those lists? I doubt it. Parenting, like gardening, involves an act of faith, a giving of oneself to the world over time.

One of the reasons I like gardening is that no boss stands over me, marking my actions as I straighten up and listen to the white-throated sparrows and the mourning doves. It's true no boss will compliment me if I do well, or sweeten my pay envelope. There is no pay, only a harvest. With the proper collaboration between John and me and the forces of nature, a teaspoon of seed will yield a bushelbasket of produce. To me, that is the best pay in the world. But I have to sweat for it.

Maybe it is the sweating for it that repels non-gardeners. Human mythology is full of contradictory stories about the origins of agriculture. In Genesis we read that God planted the first garden in Eden and left Adam "to dress it and keep it." In other words, God had done the heavy work first. After Adam and Eve are turned out of Eden, God tells Adam, "In the sweat of thy face shalt thou eat bread." In this account, work is a punishment. In Celtic mythology are plants that seed themselves, ploughs that plough on their own.

But in other accounts, agriculture is a divine gift. The Greeks worshipped the goddess Athena because she taught them how to cultivate the olive tree. The American Indians worshipped corn deities.

At a certain point of my life the notion of sitting on my behind while the trees bore fruit for me and the plants seeded themselves and the magical ploughs opened magical furrows would have been very appealing. But not anymore, somehow. A little sweat never hurt anybody, and it flushes out the soul as well as the pores.

Gardening is a collaboration with nature, and perhaps the people who are not repelled by the sweat of gardening are repelled by feeling that they can't dominate the earth, whip it into line, make it mind. Certainly the ads for herbicide and pesticide, with their hairy-voiced announcers and their promise of miraculous yields, conjure up pictures of clean-nailed farmers in leisure suits who sit on their verandas watching their land convert itself painlessly into money. But all growers of whatever scale know that, though they give their plants the best start in life and the best care along the way, they do not make the plants grow. The plants grow on their own, like the lilies of the field that Jesus commended to his disciples' attention. In this conjunction of earth and sun and air and seed-stuff, a life power existed before we did and survives our wars and hatreds. The grass covers our old battlefields and indifferently veils the grave of the martyr and the assassin. Is it by chance that the attitude of prayer is also the attitude of the planter?

Nor is gardening a solitary triumph. The corn I plant came to me through a long line of human hands: seed companies and extension agronomists, ladies with kitchen gardens, farmers with broad acres, a German monk who uncovered the secrets of genetic selection through twenty years in a monastery garden, Indian women who planted and bred for thousands of years before ever a white man sank tooth into those golden kernels. The first known corn was about the size of a head of oats and each kernel had an individual husk. What we have now comes from all those thousands of years of dedication, the earth opening itself, the planters bending to seed it. Each generation writing, with hope but without arrogance, its own signature on the brown sheet of earth, kneeling down before the mysteries of growth, earning its bread in the sweat of its brow.

ST. CLOUD TIMES

Picking Rock

May 19, 1982

John and Eric have picked some rock this spring, and one day Eric hired himself out to a neighbor for a day of rock picking. So far, they haven't needed my services. I don't know whether to feel good or bad about this. I've got lots of other things to do, and, no doubt about it, rock picking is hard work. On the other hand, there have been times when I've enjoyed picking rock.

I especially remember a day in early June a couple of years ago when we picked rock in the soybean field. The soybeans were big enough to be visible, small enough for the truck to straddle the rows without damage. It was a good day for the job—warm but with a breeze. The four of us, John and I and Shireen and Eric, moved out acoss the field to pick up the stones, every size from baseball up to basketball. We used pitchforks to help loosen the ones partly sunk in the ground; a few stones that were tombstone size we left for another day. We moved the truck forward a little when we had cleared a section of field. When we were done, we carried our near-truckload of rocks over to the house and dumped most of them into the foundation footings for what is now our greenhouse.

I suppose rock picking must be as old as agriculture, at least in any rocky soil. Most of Minnesota was glacier country once, and glaciers leave not only lakes but rocks behind them. Frost brings rocks to the surface. No matter how many are picked each year, there always seems to be more next year. And when there's nothing else to do on the farm and the fields are open, one can always pick rock.

Picked rock is traditionally loaded onto a stone boat. I blinked several times the first time I heard the words "stone boat." Of course a stone boat isn't a boat made of stone, but a wheelless drag pulled by a tractor or, in the old days, by horses. But lots of people pick into pickups. Or they use a tractor pulling a hayrack or an old car hood equipped with chains and inverted.

Though there are mechanical rock pickers on the market, most rock picking is still not fully mechanized. As a result, it is somewhat communal and social: family units do it or half a dozen kids. Like hay baling, it produces a certain mild exhibitionism among the young, especially in warm weather. Boys strip to the waist "to keep cool." Girls wear shorts and halter-tops "to get a tan." Once I saw a young lady picking rock in a bright red bikini— sensible shoes on the feet, sensible chore gloves on the hands, not much between but bare young girl.

I've never heard any work songs for picking rock like the songs for and about picking and chopping cotton and hoeing corn. But John's maternal grandfather, a Swedish immigrant like all four of his grandparents, used to recite Norse sagas to his children while they picked rock.

The stone fences in Robert Frost's poem "Mending Wall" were undoubtedly an end product of rock picking. Maybe because a lot of Minnesota was broken to the plow after the introduction of barbed wire, we have no tradition of stone fences. But older barns sometimes have fieldstone foundations, and the hunting lodges wealthy men built for themselves up here in the twenties have fieldstone fireplaces.

Most fields in central Minnesota have piles of rocks in the corner, but these piles are nothing compared to the rock piles further north. Up in the pine country of Northern Minnesota, after the lumber companies cut off the white and Norway pines, land-hungry settlers bought cheap or homesteaded. Where the soil was stony, people have left permanent monuments, like crumbling fortifications—those great mounds and dikes of rock that they had cleared from their fields stone by stone. Some homesteaders are still there, managing in a country of short summers and forty-below winters. More have fought a losing battle trying to wring corn and rye and rutabagas and cream checks out of thin soil and have lost out to jack pines that retake land cleared by fire or the axe. The log cabins and barns and the saunas of the Finns have crumbled away or have been buried in the brush, and almost nothing shows that anyone ever lived there but the nomadic Chippewa. A friend once showed me his grandparents' home farm, now in the Chippewa National Forest; nothing was left of the homesite but a well casing.

It's not possible to be too melancholy about those vanished farms. When the same land will grow straggly, yellow-leaved, waist-high corn or luxuriant hundred-and-fifty-foot trees, there is not much question about which crop better suits it. Most of that land is better growing what it now grows: pine and poplar and grouse and blueberries and white-tailed deer.

LONG PRAIRIE LEADER

A Dance to Old Music

May 23, 1988

Walking behind my husband, I drop three kernels of corn into each of the holes he has dug.

It is a lovely spring morning, this day we make our first planting of corn. The tiny green beads on the trees are beginning to unfold into leaves. The woods around our garden, which last week showed mostly bare limbs, are now veiled in green. Another few days and the billowing shade of full leaf-out will flow up hill and down dale. As I reach into the sack of seed and pick out the hard kernels, three by three, I can hear robins, red-winged blackbirds, and the phoebe which is building a nest above the living room window in Birch House. Yesterday, for the first time in three springs, I heard the song of the white-throated sparrow.

We have a corn-planter with which we could do this job. A blocky, narrow box that is filled with corn and swung forward, letting the end of it chunk into the ground, pressing the handles to drop the seed into the prepared soil. But this garden is being planted in a hillside, and we want to do everything we can to keep its rather thin topsoil from washing downhill. My husband has dug the holes for the corn so that each one has a little hillock on the downhill side. Each row we have planted has a small terrace to catch the rain.

After I drop the seed, I scrape the soft earth in, careful not to flatten the erosion-preventing hillock.

Eleven thousand years ago, this hillside was a pile of raw, glacier-dumped rock. Forests form topsoils, I have read, at an average rate of two inches per thousand years. But I imagine that's on flat ground. This hillside was full of young, vigorous hop horn beam and ironwood trees when we cleared it three springs ago, but it was hardly virgin soil, and it is not deep. Clearing away timber, which we had to do if we were going to garden, left it exposed to the rain, and, though we quickly planted it to oats that first year and let it lie fallow the second, we have lost some of that precious dark tilth already. So I press down gently, not disturbing the hillocks.

Soil needs to be firmed over newly planted seed. My instinct is always to fold the soil in as if I were covering a newborn baby. I have to remind myself to press down firmly, as I always have to remind myself, later, to thin thoroughly. Plants needn't be handled brutally, but sometimes they need to be firmly dealt with.

When I was a child, my grandmother told me about the Indian women who came to plant potatoes in her mother's garden. That must have been on what was then the Canadian frontier when her father was a missionary. These Indian women would plant the potatoes and press down the soil with their moccasins, each leaving an identifying mark. Each woman would take her pay in the form of a certain number of hills of potatoes, in proportion to what she had planted.

I wish I had asked for more details about this story. When I was a child, it was simply one of Grandma's stories, happening in the great "once upon a time, long, long ago" where all good stories happen. As an adult I would have asked all sorts of questions. What year was this? What tribe were these Indians? How many were there? Did they bring their children with them? And, especially, how could the scuff marks of moccasin-soles last through the rain and weeds of a whole summer?

Grandma has been dead since 1946. Perhaps if I had asked my father, he might have remembered some of those details, but he died in 1970. So I will never know. But as I plant and step, plant and step, I remember both my grandmother and those Indian women, so long dead.

As I move along the row, across the hill-slope, the drop, scrape, and stomp make a slow, functional, but elegant dance to the fine old music of the robins and phoebes. It is a dance and a music that has been going on for a long time.

The Book of Genesis tells me this planting dance is punishment for the sin of disobedience. It was because they had eaten the forbidden fruit that Adam and Eve were driven from God's garden to earn their bread by the sweat of their brow.

If this work is punishment for sin, why do I enjoy it so much? There's the white throat again.

I'm done with this planting of corn. On to the squash.

MORRISON COUNTY RECORD

Mortar

August 10, 1987

For a literary person, I seem to spend an awful lot of time with mortar on my hands.

Getting my hands dirty is nothing new. Even an artist of the most delicate sensibility would have a tough time raising a family without getting a little dirt on the hands. Then there are the garden and the livestock, begun as exercises in thrift and Thoreauvian self-sufficiency, which quickly became passions. Ditto the fireplace and the woodburning stove, for which firewood has to be cut, hauled out of the woods, split, carried into the house and fed to the firebox. Of course the ashes come out later too, to join the compost or be spread on the garden.

The house in which I'm now living was built fourteen years ago by my husband, with assistance from the children and from me too. But then, most of what I did was gophering—go for this, go for that. It hadn't occurred to me that I would ever, *could* ever, do construction beyond handing things to the carpenter. Writers are supposed to be specialists in literary, not literal, construction. Besides, building things is "Man's Work."

The house in which I am living is a beautiful house. It is also a large house. Having three children, with an eight-year age span among them, it is handy to have four bedrooms, a rec room, and a greenhouse. But with the children gone, is it logical to heat and cool and maintain and clean a house twice as big as two people need?

It will cost a pang to see these massive beams, which I have always loved, these rooms, where my children grew up, belong to somebody else.

On the other hand, we have some new ideas about the kind of home we want, and we are busy carrying them out, which is where the mortar comes in.

Specifically, I have been laying up cordwood masonry. Peeled, dried log-ends are mortared together. When the builder does the job right, the wall that results combines the texture and charm of wood with the sturdiness of masonry.

Once I started counting up all the ancillary construction assistance I've provided over the past year, I was surprised at how long and complicated the list got. Stacking wood. Unstacking wood. Sanding and staining and painting wood. Hauling water. Screening sand. Shoveling sand for the cement mixer, six buckets to the load of cement, a job that leaves the shoveler feeling like a letter L turned on its side. All real work. All necessary.

But now I look at a section of wall and know that I built it, with these two female, literary hands.

Why do it? Why should anybody build his or her own place when whole industries devote themselves to building *for* people? That question is a variant on the one that hardly anybody asks me anymore but which I know they must think from time to time. Why do we grow our own food? Supermarkets are full of it.

Part of the answer for us now, as it was twenty-three years ago when we moved from California suburbia to rural Minnesota, is the echo of Henry Thoreau's "simplify, simplify" ringing in our heads. Another part is remembering something my mother-in-law said once when I scolded her for lugging heavy buckets of water up a hillside in the heat. "You let people start doing things for you," Mother said, "and pretty soon you can't do them for yourself."

Simplicity, self-sufficiency, and doing things yourself are ideas to which a lot of people pay lip service. Complexity, dependence, and pre-fabrication are the order of the day, whether we are talking houses, food, ideas, or lives. Rich and poor, West and East, capitalist and socialist, everybody is moving toward the assembly line and the microchip and away from the hoe and the trowel. Those countries that haven't yet made the shift to industrialization—places where some people still provide their own food, clothing, and shelter from their own land—are called underdeveloped countries.

I am not silly enough to think that we will stem this flood toward specialization by mortaring up our own walls. But at least this writer has learned a few things about how buildings are put together and learned to appreciate good workmanship, too. I look at mortar with a different eye now that I've got it under my nails.

Altogether too many journalists in this country sit on their tailored rumps, telling workers to produce more and settle for less, telling farmers to quit bellyaching. I can't help thinking that all of us would be better off if those guys prepared for their pontifications by shoveling a little manure—the literal, animal-derived substance—and getting some mortar on their hands.

MORRISON COUNTY RECORD

The Land Endures

November 5, 1986

Now the leaves, which were green canopies and veils all summer and glowing banners for the brief weeks of early fall, all come
rustling down. I walk to the garden, shuffling through leaves, making more noise than I have to for the sheer pleasure of hearing that
crisp crunch-crunch. It will not last long. Frost and rain and the
first work of fungi, and these leaves will be soft brown rags, quickly
lost in the crumbling blackness of leaf-mold.

Frost is predicted. We pick the peppers, haul in the squash,
pick all the tomatoes that have changed color. I'm getting a little
tired of canning tomatoes. My greenhouse windows are already
full of tomatoes ripening slowly between layers of newspaper.
But it would be wasteful just to let the frost have them. So we
cover as much as we can.

Soon all but the stubborn leaves of the red oak will go, and
the hard, defined shapes of hills and fields and junked farm machinery will stand out again, till the snow covers them. A season
of growth will be packed away with the canned tomatoes, the potatoes and carrots and beets and rutabagas in their buckets of sand,
the corn in the bins, the stacked hay, the chopped silage.

Our transactions with the land start as soon as it's thawed
and warm in spring. Disc the garden, rake it, plant it, weed and

cultivate it, pick and process the produce, compost the waste to be plowed back in and start the process over. This is the cycle, the theory. In practice, every year has its different, specific memories of weeding and hoeing, praying for rain and then for sun, whole-souled delight and heartfelt cursing. Between freezing and canning and storing we will have enough vegetables for dinners, enough juice for breakfasts, to last us till the asparagus and rhubarb of next spring. Throw in the twenty-five chicks we raised from peeping babyhood to freezer readiness, the two steers and three lambs well-padded with summer grass, and we can feed ourselves. (All but the exotic substances, like coffee.)

If there's a certain melancholy to saying good-bye to summer, there's also a certain satisfaction in being done with it. Good-bye, faithful and sturdy peas that kept bearing into October. Good-bye, worst crop of squash I ever raised. Good-bye, incredibly prolific broccoli, skimpy cantaloupe, heavy purple eggplants, little green tomatoes that will be white and flabby after frost. Good-bye, dark soil that I planned to keep tidy as a frame around my beds and rows but which wound up hairy with weeds. Good-bye, successes and failures of 1986. Sleep well under your drifts of leaves and snow. I'll see you again next spring.

Human beings started out in a relationship with nature that had to be close and observant. Our ancestors found out that the earth could feed them, but only if they were clever and watchful. They learned where the edible plants grew and when they were ripe and how they could be preserved, how animals could be caught, how the waters could yield their fish and the skies their birds. In time they learned to take the productivity of the earth into their own hands, to make the plants grow where they wanted them, to turn the wild ox who roars in fierce splendor from cave paintings into the gentle cow who lets herself be milked by human hands and gives us her calves for dinner. Agriculture was the beginning of all other culture, good and evil.

Now we have cut ourselves loose from the soil, and most Americans, even "nature-loving" Americans, relate to the earth much as if it were scenery they look at through car windows on a trip. They may think it's pretty, but they have no sense of responsibility for it, no fellow-feeling.

For all the times I've gotten sunburned hoeing, for all those tomatoes yet to can, I count it among the great, good fortunes of a successful life to have learned to live *with* the earth, not just on it. And as I put my garden to bed, I am thinking with sorrow of those people who look out over fields they won't cultivate again.

Yes, the economics of farm failure is important. So is the politics. I've written about both before, and I will again. But as I say good-bye for now to my own good piece of fertile ground, I think of farm families for whom this fall is a last good-bye. I wish them well, I wish them good jobs, I pray they can hang on to their sense of themselves as worthwhile people, good people who did not fail but were caught in the economic machinery of our cruel, complicated age. I hope they can find lives as good as they are losing—though that will be hard.

I just want to say that I know how they feel as they look at the earth with which, by which, and for which they have lived, and which they are leaving through no choice of their own.

The land endures, though good men and women leave it. The earth endures in her beauty and variety and will bloom and bear again next year.

LONG PRAIRIE LEADER

Seasons

Living in this part of the world,
it's impossible to ignore the seasons
even if we wanted to.
Which we don't.

March

March 19, 1986

Between the silver woods and fields of winter and the greening woods and fields of spring comes March.

That is, in years when spring is normal—whatever normal means in this state. I have vivid memories of my first March in Minnesota. I was living in an uninsulated, wood-heated, unplumbed lakeside cottage. The year was 1965. An intensely cold, very snowy winter was topped off by massive blizzards, the first beginning on March 1 and the second on March 17. After the St. Patrick's Day blizzard that year, it took three days to clear major roads, two more before we got a tractor in to scoop out our access road. It snowed on April 3, my birthday. There were still four-foot walls of snow along our driveway in mid-April. It even snowed a few flakes on Memorial Day.

All the springs since then have seemed to me like a piece of cake.

More typically, March means grimy, slumping snow, puddles, the beginning of warm-up, interspersed here and there with winter's last whacks, like the fabled State Basketball Tournament Blizzard. Meteorologist Bruce Watson has written, "If you have a friend in California or Florida you would like to have visit and gain a favorable impression of Minnesota, do not invite that person here in March. The only kind of person that could be fascinated by

March is a meteorologist. . . ."

Still, a lot of fascinating stuff goes on in March, and I don't mean just all those picturesque road boils. That hypothetical visitor from Florida or California, alternately slopping and shivering, might find it odd to see so many smiling faces on Minnesota streets in March. But after the long cold of winter, it just feels so good to be able to walk around outside without long johns. Without a hat! Maybe even, for a daring short time, with the jacket unzipped!

All that grime of March—the dirty snow, the puddles, the wafts of thawing manure piles in country places—signals the turn of the year, the end of hibernation, life starting over. In midnight barns, hogs are farrowing, ewes are lambing. On thousands of window sills, little pots accumulate. Tucked into their soil are the tiny nuggets of germ plasm which will become flowers and cabbages, peppers and tomatoes. March comes in scrawny and smeared and bawling, like a newborn baby.

Some years—not all—March means maple sugaring. Sap begins to run when night temperatures are below freezing, day temperatures above it. During the last few years, our March has meant the "tink-tink" of sap dropping into buckets, the roar of a well-fed fire, the smell of wood smoke and clear maple sap boiling down to golden-brown syrup.

All this mixes with the smells of sheep manure and wool and lamb milk replacer, with small plaintive bleats of newborn lambs and little responding mutters of their dams. And the whole symphony of sounds, smells, sensations filtered through heavy fatigue. In lambing time, human sleep comes second, a lesson I have never forgotten since I once dawdled out to the barn and found a ewe past helping. Assisting at the birth process is hard work, sometimes sad work. It's not only money gone when a dead lamb is carried out; there are the perfectly formed little bones, the soft hooves, the peppercorn wool, the mouth that can't bleat or suckle hanging open, the clever little tongue going cold as an icicle. And the shepherd with no magic wand to wave.

Yet when it's all over—the last ewe delivered, the last bottle lamb old enough to fend for itself, the last spiles pulled from the maples, and the buckets and sap cooker cleaned up—and I've looked back, recalling it all, what a vivid and intensely-felt season it's been! Nobody could have given me that experience. I could not have bought it at a store or a travel agency. It had to be earned. Working hard, dealing with life and death, pushing past some personal limit, one is probably not always happy, but *is* alive right down to the last brain cell and the marrow of the bones.

So here comes March, in like a lamb this year, and we all know what that means. March, with potholes and slop, runny noses, muddy carpets. March, when my now-grown oldest used to dig canals in the driveway mud and melt water by the hour, loving thaw and slop because then he could make "waterways." March, and the winter house air suddenly dead, let's open a window here even if it is only forty-five degrees! March, and the cry of geese and tundra swans heading north.

The calendar says that January begins the new year. But March beings the year of growth and new life.

LONG PRAIRIE LEADER

June

June 15, 1981

It's time to stop whatever we're doing and just be—just live and breathe and feel, just see and hear. We are in the middle of one of the great, glorious experiences of human life. We are in the middle of June in Minnesota.

June in Minnesota is what most of us dream when we dream of tropical paradises—Hawaii or Tahiti. June is warm, but not too warm. Warm enough to wear loose clothes, to get a tan, to work up a pleasant glow toward the middle of the day. Warm enough to lie down without blankets and let the soft air off the lake ripple over us like some magic balm designed to ease away every pain and release every tension.

June is green and blossoming. In June everything grows. The bare brown fields of May shimmer with the silver-green pelt of oats, the stiff squadrons of corn. The pea and bean seeds shoulder up through the cultivated earth. The bedding plants come out of their flats, grow some roots, begin to flourish and bloom. As my mother-in-law is fond of saying "some days things grow just as if they're being pulled out of the ground."

And everything in June is new. Everywhere are spotty-breasted robins—the first spring hatch—and small-sized red squirrels and garden-menacing numbers of rabbits that seem to have climbed out of an Easter basket and shed their coconut fur. Kids let out of school want to try everything at once—bikes, fishing rods, skates, swim suits. June is a month for both the pomp and circumstance of graduations and weddings and the cut-off and tee-shirt casualness of cookouts and picnics. Even the stuffiest people take off their ties in June.

Of course there is drama in June, and exasperation, and even sometimes tragedy. June is a fine month for thunderstorms. As a dramatic performance, the blossoming of cumulus clouds into the familiar thundercloud-anvil and the subsequent light and sound show with natural amplification is more exciting than any rock concert. Watching dry fields refresh themselves is lovely; walking out afterwards, pouring an inch of water out of the rain gauge, admiring the glint of drops on leaves and watching the last of the rainbow fade is enough to make me feel life is worth living, however many bills we have gotten in the day's mail. But there is a dark side to all this. People do get hit by lightning. The lush fields of oats get pounded flat by hail. Tornadoes are real, not just pieces of excitement on the news. And it is true that bugs and weeds grow just as fast as birds and blossoms.

And then, too, June goes by so fast. Before we have taken a deep breath, the last peony and iris have gone to join the lilac and the apple blossoms. The wild geraniums wither and the first oxeye daisies open. The first incredible luminous fresh green, the miraculous transition from bare boughs to dappled shade, becomes ordinary, like a wall seen a thousand times. The leaves grow dusty and insect-chewed. Heat intensifies over the summer fields. The kids get bored, they watch television in the middle of the day, they whine, "There's nothin' to do!" Everything needs to be weeded or thinned or canned or frozen at once. There won't be time for all the projects. Someone has left a wet bathing suit on the floor for the hundredth time; it smells of dog-day algae and mildew. The cicadas are singing. The staghorn sumac is red. There is a gold leaf on the basswood.

Surely somewhere, in Hawaii or Tahiti or paradise, there are no bugs or weeds, the hail spares the oats, nobody's house is exploded all over the ten o'clock news. Surely somewhere the radiance of June is forever new, yet permanent. Surely somewhere we can have apple blossoms and lilacs, peonies and wild roses all at once.

But half the beauty of June is in the long days, which seem to last forever and yet are gone in a blink. The killdeer nesting in our cornfield, the one which did the broken-wing trick to lure us away from her nest, that killdeer has gone, and her four spotted eggs have grown legs and wings, and even the shells are gone. Nothing is left but the saucer of pebbles and twigs on the brown earth.

There is a beauty of the young and new—the child on the swing, the bride looking through her veil—a hopeful virginal beauty. There is another beauty of experiences—the beauty of the men and women watching the ceremony, the faces that have seen a few things, the bodies that have been knocked around a little by the world. There is the beauty of the first blossom and the beauty of the full crop pouring into the bin and the beauty of the barn full of quiet life, steaming among the frozen fields where the dormant roots and seeds wait under the snow. Each is the climax of something and the beginning of something else. Maybe somewhere else it all stands still, holds, is forever the same. Probably not Hawaii or Tahiti, maybe paradise. The beauty of this world is the beauty of flow.

Stop! Stop to live and breathe and hear. It's June in Minnesota.

MORRISON COUNTY RECORD

There Is a Season

September 1, 1991

The first faint traces of gold can now be seen in the trees, as if someone with a fine brush has been gilding the edges of the leaves.

I don't know whether the hummingbirds are visiting the feeders more often, stoking themselves for the trip to Costa Rica where they winter, or whether I only think so because I know that they will be gone soon. Birds, including hummingbirds, have been migrating for millennia, and presumably the hummingbirds find nothing remarkable in a trip from Grey Eagle across the American continent and the Gulf of Mexico to the winter range. They don't even do it in flocks but singly. And, of course, the young of this year will never have made the trip before.

The monarch butterflies, slow drifts of black-and-gold wings across the late summer sky, are already heading south. They move individually, but there are so many of them that we often have fourteen or fifteen in our front yard. They winter in Mexico, where none of them have ever been. They were all hatched out in Minnesota and grew up in their larval stages munching Minnesota milkweed.

Drifting south, some of them will migrate eighteen hundred miles. They will overwinter in Mexico, head north with spring, stop along the way to deposit their eggs, then die. Their children, at least one generation—and sometimes more—removed from the fields of central Minnesota, will come fluttering back next spring.

It is a season of change, but then every season, properly considered, is a season of change. "To everything there is a season, and a time to every purpose under the heaven," begins a beautiful passage in the book of Ecclesiastes.

The human race has been thinking about change (which is to say, about time) for a long time with mixed reactions. Little kids get fixated on a particular pattern of behavior—same book, same toy, same demand for a drink of water—and woe betide the bored or tired or hurried parent who tries to change the pattern around. Then along about age twelve they discover the word "boring" and spend at least a decade complaining about the wearisome routine of their lives. (I'm sure even the adolescent children of traveling lion tamers and rock-and-roll performers complain bitterly that their lives are "boring.")

At the civic, corporate, national level, humans seem fascinated with changing things, moving dirt and water and vegetation around. We like to leave our mark on the landscape, gathering stones (and cement and plastic and dams and overpasses and office buildings) together on a grand scale. At the personal level, change is more painful.

Sometimes it seems as if we just learn how to do something when we are forced to learn how to do something else. Just when we get really comfortable with putting on our own clothes and taking care of ourselves in the bathroom and riding our trikes, and they shoot us off to school to learn a whole new bunch of stuff. Just when we're comfortable with milk money and bicycles, and all of a sudden we're expected to be teenagers and know about cars and dating. Just get to where we figure we have the hang of adolescence, and they throw us out of school and expect us to get a job and raise a family.

It doesn't get any easier after that. Get good at a job, and we get promoted. Learn how to take pretty good care of a houseful of kids, and one fine day we look around, and the place is empty. Get competent at the business of middle age, and one day we're old—

To everything there is a season. The trees and the hummingbirds and the monarch butterflies take it all as it comes, including "A time to be born, and a time to die." Humans find that a little difficult.

The first gold is in the trees. The hummingbirds are getting ready to go south.

Winter Sky

October 25, 1982

A few more leaves come down every day. Every day a little more of the heavens becomes visible.

I'm writing this column on a grey, cold, windy day. The temperature has been hanging at around forty degrees since I got up this morning and doesn't seem likely to go any higher. The tree nearest my window, a maple, is hanging on to its last hundred leaves, which have lost their earlier golden color and are brown. At intervals, one lets go and whips away down the wind. The day may very well end with the first snowfall of 1982. It is not the sort of day about which chambers of commerce like to brag.

It's easy to get romantically gloomy about the bare trees of late fall. Indeed, some people regularly get gloomy in the fall as a matter of policy. My friend, the lady who lives up the hill, for all the years I've known her, has greeted the fall color-change in the trees with a head-shaking, foreboding pronouncement, "You hate to see it come."

Having said that, having gotten the gloom off her chest, she gets on with the winter business of ample meals, big logs on the fire, and Thanksgiving family gatherings. Summer parties and picnics are fun, but hospitality has its keenest edge in the winter.

Some of my happiest memories of childhood are of coming

37

home from school on cold, nasty days and coming into the light
and the warmth and the wonderful smell of good food cooking.
Homemade soup on the back of the stove! Homemade rolls rising
where my mother always put the pan to catch the warmth, up on
top of the old, black, curlicued family piano! And, if Mom felt especially sympathetic toward the frozen wayfarer, a cup of cocoa
with marshmallows! Nobody can tell me that eating in the fanciest
fifty-dollar lunch, snob-gourmet joint in New York has quite the
same thrill as thawing out red, pickly fingers around a cup of hot
cocoa at the kitchen table when you're ten.

In summer there is no hard line between inside and outside.
The doors and windows are open, the sounds and smells of summer
come in, and the kids run in and out like squirrels chasing each
other around a tree. Most of the hard lines of the world are ob-
scured also. Houses are hidden, tree shapes are half-concealed,
rolling country blurs off in a mist of green. Now the doors and
windows are shut, the leaves are down, the hills and trees stand
naked; I see my neighbors' houses, and they can see mine. The
pleasant summer illusion of living alone and for ourselves gives
place to the consciousness that we are part of a community.

And over it all, when the clouds clear, is the immense unen-
cumbered sky, to tell us we are part of something bigger than our
neighborhood. The light of stars, which left home thousands of
years ago, shines down on the barn where the breath of calves
and sheep steams and on the house where our labor keeps a family
warm and fed. The sky of winter is not warm and diaphanous
like the summer sky. It isn't cruel, either. It is just out there, bigger
than us.

Some people cannot stand this bigness. Beret in Ole Rolvag's
novel of pioneer immigrant life, *Giants in the Earth*, goes mad out
on the plains of western Minnesota. It is all too big and too strange.
She has left her parents and the places she knows in Norway. Surely
this strange country is the Devil's place, not God's. And mostly
she cannot stand the empty, treeless landscape, the empty, open
sky. There is no place to hide. There must have been a lot of lonely
Berets out on the frontier, alone all winter without television,
radio, telephone, car, mail service—all that network of human
messages that ties us together and keeps us from floating loose
down the wind, like the last leaves from my window maple.

Other people are exalted by that bigness. Three of the world's
major religions, Judaism, Christianity, and Islam, all came to
expression in desert countries among partly nomadic people,
people who lived under the immense sky of the desert. And the

Greeks who gave us so much of the philosophical underpinnings of western culture were great seafarers. They knew the sky as it shows itself to voyagers, all around them, not cut off from them by walls or trees.

There were, and have been throughout history, men and women who were happiest in this deep communion with the heavens and the heavenly, who came in for cups of cocoa only now and then and with a certain reluctance. And there were and are plenty of Berets, too. Modern Berets tend not to go mad. They tend to drive everywhere and build roofs over everything. In their more grandiose moments they talk about doming whole cities. And about weather control. No more grey days, no more sharp, fall winds, no more mud and sleet and blizzards. No more infinite sky.

When I think of this prospect of a paved, roofed, comfortable, unchallenging world, I think of Henry Thoreau, who said about late fall, "The woods, divested in great part of their leaves, are being ventilated. It is the season of perfect works, of hard, tough, ripe twigs, not of tender buds and leaves. The leaves have made their wood, and a myriad new withes stand up all around pointing to the sky, able to survive the cold. It is only the perennial that you see, the iron age of the year." I am reminded also of the Navajo Indian names for the earth, which differ from season to season. The earth, to the Navajo, is Changing Woman. In summer, with her soft leaves and skies, she is Changing Woman Happiness. But in winter, in the iron age of the year, she is Changing Woman Long Life.

MORRISON COUNTY RECORD

Early Winter

November 7, 1991

For purposes of column writing, I wish I could narrate some exciting things that happened to me during the Halloween Storm of the Century. Unfortunately, the most exciting thing I did was sort the books in my living room (a task that had me feeling guilty because I had put it off for months) and finish a chapter in the novel I'm writing. And listen to the wind scream. Normally we can hardly hear anything in our earth-sheltered house, but for forty-eight hours the wind roared steadily.

No doubt about it, this year we have winter—not fall but full-scale winter—about a month earlier than normal. Our woods are deep in snow, probably too deep to melt till sometime in April.

There are things I enjoy about winter. I love the smell of wood smoke and the crackle of flames. I love the billows of white giving elegance to the bare sticks in the woods. Spring will mean gardening again, and I'm fond of my garden, but the proposition of gardening twelve months out of the year does not appeal to me. I like the quiet of winter, the chance to do serious extended writing, the chance to catch up on my reading (which will be easier, now that I have sorted those books).

Many people find winter very depressing. They miss the sun. They hate to drive on icy roads. They resent having to bundle up before they go outside. Even people like me, who basically like winter, sometimes find it a little long.

Psychiatrists talk about the Reality Principle—the bare-bones facts of life, against which our dreams and illusions too often rub. Winter in Minnesota, especially when the sky is grey, settles down over the state like a huge box, an embodied, four- or five-month-long Reality Principle. The bare twigs shake in the wind, and the things they say sound like an endless torrent of the kind of advice we would just as soon ignore.

Advice like: dress sensibly. Forget the high heels and the swirly dresses. You will need boots for the drifts, a thick sensible coat, double socks and pants and gloves, a hat, and probably a scarf. Skip any of these necessary precautions, and the cold will find every gap in your clothing and stab in like daggers of ice. Remember, people lose their toes to frostbite. People die of hypothermia.

Don't drive like a maniac! All it takes is one jerk of the wheel on icy roads to roll the car. No horsing around behind the wheel. No Jimmy Rockford stunts. And don't forget the sleeping bag in the back seat, the emergency kit, the bucket of sand, and the jumper cables.

Caution is also the watchword when it comes to walking. Forget about striding. Adopt the prudent, wide-based, short-stepping Minnesota shuffle. You may look like a penguin as you scuttle down the street all wrapped up in down and wool. But everybody looks kind of round in appropriate winter clothes, and better to look silly then to spend the winter in traction. And while we're thinking about it, better lay in a supply of cold remedies and consider getting flu shots. It's winter, you know.

I remember saying those things, or some of those things, to my children and throwing up my hands in despair as they rushed out of the house in sneakers and jeans and an unzipped jacket. I don't understand how they avoided frostbite amputation and pneumonia.

But I don't enjoy constantly being reminded by the weather of all the catastrophic things that can happen to a person, either. Winter just seems to take all the slack out of life, all the looseness, all the possibility for error. (So do the jungle and the desert, but those of us who live in Minnesota rarely travel in those tropical climes.)

Notice how the ads for cruise ships always show young people with beautiful bodies cavorting in swimming pools and dance halls and casinos. If we think about it, we know perfectly well that people on cruises get seasick and sunburned, are subject to all the travel miseries of lost luggage, boring companions, and astronomic expenses, and do not automatically look like Cathy Lee just because they bought the ticket for the cruise. Those images are only peripherally related to the actual experience of travel in warm climes (just as snowmobile and ski vacation ads always show a wonderland of perfect snow, without engine breakdowns or fractured shins). Such ads cater to our desire for a world in which life, in Ernest Hemingway's phrase, is a constant fiesta.

Of course, as the cold, grey winter sky reminds us, everybody's life consists of far more work and struggle and sorrow and adversity than it does joy. People who really expect life to be a continuous fiesta are in for severe disappointment. People who insist on living as if life is a continuous fiesta are uncommonly hard on their parents, friends, spouses, and children.

My goodness, now I'm talking like the Reality Principle or the winter wind myself! Enough! Just because I sorted my books while the wind screamed, I don't have to be so all-fired smug.

And it is true, as it is always true, that the cold and snow of winter is preparation and protection for the amazing fiesta of spring.

MORRISON COUNTY RECORD

Getting into Harness

December 1982

All over Minnesota, people are taking a deep breath and slipping into the Christmas harness.

The idea of getting into harness, like a workhorse or an experienced reindeer, is on the face of it slightly depressing. Is not the joy of Christmas a divine gift? On the other hand, last week's Record Gift Guide did print 137 recipes for Christmas goodies of different kinds, if my count is correct. Probably nobody will make all 137, but the length of the list certainly suggests that the joy of Christmas does include eating and drinking and that somewhere along the line somebody will have slipped into the Christmas harness so that food and drink can get to the ultimate consumers. A gentleman I know always includes in his table grace the phrase, "Bless the hands that have prepared it." This blessing is rarely so appreciated as at Christmas.

Every year people shake their heads and say, "The Christmas decorations are up already, and it's not even Thanksgiving. Why do they have to rush the season so?" I used to feel that way too, when I was young enough that my Christmas preparations consisted of buying four or five presents and maybe cracking a few nuts for my mother and helping to grind the carrots and potatoes and suet for the Christmas pudding. It's a little different now that

I have meals to cook and company for whom to prepare, Christmas cards to send and gifts to give to an expanding list of people. Thanksgiving is not at all too early to slip into harness.

First, Christmas cards. I look forward to Christmas letters, so, logically, I have to write Christmas letters. Then the house.

There's no way a person can roast a turkey without opening the oven. Others will probably be in the kitchen when that oven door is opened too. For myself, I can perfectly well live with the Black Hole, as long as my oven incrustations do not contain too much dripping from rhubarb pie. (Rhubarb pie juice heating to 350 degrees will readily drive anyone out into ten below weather just for a breath of fresh air.) But somehow I don't want all my guests going home saying, "Did you look at the inside of her oven?" So, spread out the [yuk] newspapers, on with the [ugh] gloves, shake up the [ish] oven cleaner, and fill the house with the one domestic smell that is really worse than rhubarb pie juice, the eye-smarting reek of old grease and new oven cleaner mingling.

Once the oven's cleaned, then on to the cupboards, to the walls, to the big platters and company dishes, and don't forget to rent the rug shampooer.

And then there's shopping. Well, we all know about shopping. The day when I could afford to let the shopping go 'till Christmas Eve is definitely over. The week before Christmas I'm always too busy to get out of the house, anyway.

And Christmas cooking. When I'm baking Christmas cookies or pies I always have a curious feeling because I can remember so well the wonderful smells and tastes of Christmas when I was a child. There is a moment when I am, simultaneously, the child gazing up at the miraculous competency of Mom with her beaters and stirring spoons and pastry brush and baster, and Mom herself. I have become the person I admired and envied when I was little. And if I can't, or shouldn't, eat all the cookies and frosting I want, which is one reason I used to envy my mother, it is nice to see myself reflected in small eyes as an impressive figure.

Of course, it's work. Often it's hard work. And there are people for whom putting on the Christmas harness means more work than joy. Every year, sure as Santa, there are newspaper and magazine articles about Christmas depression. A lot of people expect to feel happier at Christmas than they wind up feeling. Part of that reason is because lots of people simply overwork. There are people who put on the harness early and never take it off for a moment. By November fifteenth, their minds are ticking even in their sleep, saying, "Christmas cards, clean the house, shopping, baking, decorate the tree" until very little joy is left in the whole performance.

Sometimes one sees whole families caught up in a kind of competitive Christmas gamesmanship. "I sent more cards than you." "I baked more cookies." "But mine were more complicated; I just worked myself to death baking mine." "I gave you a twenty-dollar present, and your present to me only cost $5.98." Is this the spirit in which the angels sang and the wise men brought gifts? No, but few of us are angels and magi. We ought to work for the pleasure of our families and friends, give without thinking of return. But, being human, we do think of return, often working to astound or impress. We load up the Christmas sleigh with more goodies and decorations and presents and bowls of punch than anybody could possibly enjoy, exhaust ourselves pulling the sleigh, then wonder why on Christmas night we have added painful feet and a headache and a general sense of let-down to the inevitable logy stomach.

In a curious way, Christmas tests us. It calls on us to love, and a lot of people find it easier to bake twelve dozen cookies and run all over town buying expensive presents than to sit down and look somebody straight in the eye and say, "I love you; you mean a lot to me." It calls on us to give for the sake of giving, and even the most generous of us wants something—a thank you, anyway. It calls on us to open our hearts, like the shepherds who heard the angel's song.

All of us know that story, the shepherds and the angel and the multitude of the heavenly host, and the message of the Divine birth, and of how they "came with haste, and found Mary, and Joseph, and the babe lying in a manger." What I've only recently wondered is, who stayed with the sheep? The shepherds were "Abiding in the field, keeping watch over their flocks by night." Perhaps the sheep were lambing, or there were predators abroad. The shepherds couldn't just have gone rushing off while the choir sang "Oh, Come, All Ye Faithful" the way we used to do it in Christmas pageants. They must have talked it over, and some of the shepherds must have stayed behind to tend the sheep while the rest went off to witness the miracle.

Thinking about Christmas, I imagine those socially responsible shepherds out there with their sheep, without any question feeling a little lonesome and put upon and let down. After the heavenly host and the message, the same old Judaean hills and the same old night wind and the same old smell of wool and sheep manure. And the sheep as dumb as children, not realizing at all what a sacrifice was being made on their behalf.

Still they stayed there and did their work, witnessing the holiness of life just by doing what was needed. Putting on the harness.

MORRISON COUNTY RECORD

Why I Like
School Closings

December 5, 1983

For some of the best dramas you don't have to buy a ticket.

The potential drama of a winter storm is often announced well in advance as a low pressure area off the Pacific Coast or a swirl of clouds over the Rockies or trailing cirrus coming in from the Dakotas. The weatherman spots and confirms it. The highway department starts issuing advisories.

The question then becomes how strong, how soon. Should we hold off on the trip? Do we need anything from the feedmill or the store? Better get in a load of wood; we may need it.

There's a communal aspect to all this. Neighbors stopping to pick up the mail, back of the car full of groceries, say cheerily, "Looks like we're in for it." Conversations begin, "How are the roads?"

We've had a couple of decent storms recently, but nothing that has been classified as a blizzard. Not like the Superbowl blizzard (easily an academy-award nominee) or the St. Patrick's Day blizzard of 1965 that snowbound us for five days in a cabin. Now those were real storms. Howling winds. Drifting snow. The disappearance of familiar landmarks. Expeditions to the barn taking on the coloring of Jerry Speis tackling the Pacific. Fighting the wind with a five-gallon bucket of water in either hand. Plunging from the sting of wind and snow into the breathing silence of the barn. The calves bawling, the sheep butting each other to get to the hay, their breaths steaming. Fine siftings of snow where wind penetrates a crack. Very hard not to feel at least moderately courageous by the time we're back in the house. The feet may be wet, the fingers cold, but the house never seemed warmer, the company never better.

Then the school closings. Some of my happiest moments have been waking up to the sound of school closings. District by district, town by town, the school closings confirm in me two important convictions. The first is that the world has not yet entirely fallen under human domination. Despite our best efforts, we haven't figured out how to convert the cosmos into a shopping mall or a battle zone. Conviction two is that I live in a sensible state. When it gets too bad to travel, Minnesotans stay home and keep the kids with them. It's rather remarkable when you think about it. At any given time, half the people in the state must be churned up about some work that needs doing. Gotta wash those walls, gotta make that sale, gotta finish that project, gotta get that presentation done. And then the snow shuts everything down. And then what? Life goes on, once the snow is shoveled away, as if nothing has been lost.

Yeah, I know. All those pictures and headlines on television calculated to make the chambers of commerce in Florida and California rub their hands together. Snow! Sleet! Minnesota Digs Out after Record Storm!

But think about those stories. Where are the crooks, the bombs, the scandals in high places, the family in collapse and the republic in danger? Not in the "Dig Out" stories. The "Dig Out" stories are full of intrepid snowplow drivers, babies delivered by anxious but successful fathers in the backs of trucks on the freeway, people who open their homes to strangers. The "Dig Out" stories are full of kindness and hospitality and foresight and courage. If I wanted to exemplify a lot of the best in America and show it to the world, I'd get a good "Dig Out" story. The readers would say, "Well, they have a lot of snow there, but, my, those people seem helpful. And friendly."

Anyway, what kind of state do we want to be? Do we want to be the home of the high roller? The place where people in search of skin cancer and a quick buck expose themselves to strangers and smog?

No, this is Minnesota, where the storms come in like a collaboration between Wagner, Barnum and Bailey, and Carl Sagan, where sensible people react to danger by shutting down the schools, holing up with their families and riding it out. This is where we half wake hearing the wind, then wake all the way to fields of sculptured whiteness, the crackle of the wood stove, the consciousness that whatever we felt we had to do can wait, and the voice of the announcer reading, "Litchfield, Little Falls public and parochial, Long Prairie, Luverne—"

MORRISON COUNTY RECORD

Family

I try to write from the ground up.
Here is the ground on which I feel the most at home,
the daily experience of living with other people.
When I first began writing columns, I had two
children at home, one in grade school, one in high school,
plus a college student coming home on weekends.
I was incredibly busy.
Being committed to writing a regular column made
a little space in my life. I hope reading it made a little
space in some other busy lives.

The Culdrum Township Time Machine

July 1, 1981

Not long ago we had dessert with Mother. (By "Mother" I mean Mother Rylander, who lives up the hill from us. My mother lives in California and is always called Mom.) Mother talked about her childhood on one of the farms her parents operated—about the day she and her brother went to cultivate with a young, frisky work team. On the logging road that went up to the field, something went wrong with the harness, and the horses ran away. "Let 'em go, Al!" she remembered crying to her brother. Now she said it at the table, in the strong, resonant voice of a girl of sixteen. "Let 'em run!"

Across the table, her grandson Eric listened with his mouth open and asked, "Then what happened?"

I knew what had happened. Mother had taken him aboard the Culdrum Township Time Machine. She had taken me on that machine many times before. Anybody can read history, can find out who won elections and lost the wars and even, if you read enough, what sugar cost fifty years earlier and what sort of things folks ate for dinner way back when. But only someone who has lived in history, lived in the world before you were in it, can take you back into that world.

I call Mother's reminiscences the Culdrum Township Time Machine because many of them center around Culdrum Township in Morrison County near Flensburg, Minnesota, where her parents lived, where she taught country school, and where her husband also grew up. But there were other places before Culdrum Township. There was the island province of Sweden called Öland, where her mother and father both grew up. There was the Swedish girl named Annette who saved her money, said good-bye to the mother she hoped to bring over to America, took the ship steerage, was one of the thousands who came through the echoing halls at Ellis Island. There was the journey to Lockport, Illinois, and the first employment as a cook and maid; the employee spoke no English, the employer no Swedish. The housewife who hired her took her out to the kitchen and showed her the flour bin, the yeast cake, and the bread pans, and she made bread. That night at dinner the master of the house solemnly tasted the new girl's bread. Then he said, speaking loudly and slowly as one does to people who don't know the language, "That's good bread, Annette!" Those must have been important words for her to hear, as she remembered them through a very long life and told her children. Mother Rylander, the eldest of her children, tells me.

There is more. The story of the father, another transplanted Swede, who worked the steel mills in the back-breaking, twelve-hour shifts of the time and married the girl from Öland. The years in Illinois, and then, when Mother was eight, the great removal to Minnesota and the first farm in Clough Township, the one on land now part of Camp Ripley. That was the farm on which the team ran away. Mother has memories of going to high school in Little Falls at thirteen. From the farm near Randall to Little Falls was a three-hour trip with workhorse and wagon. She had to rent in town, living in a room that she kept clean for herself, cooking for herself, hauling her own wood and water. In 1923 she had scarlet fever and had to stay in the pest house, a little annex to St. Gabriel's Hospital in Little Falls, not able to visit her parents when they made the long trip in, only able to talk with them through the window. She was the only patient in the pest house at the time, she remembers, and the nurse who attended her was close to her own age. As she got better, she and the nurse had pillow fights.

There are an infinity of trips to make on Mother's Time Machine, up, down, sideways. I am glad Eric took that one trip on it; I hope he will take more. I hope he will learn formal history too, for no one really understands the world in which he lives without some notion of the world it grew out of. But it's good for him to go beyond the books, to see history as ordinary people who ate and drank and loved and suffered and endured, all while inhabiting that strange time dimension—the past. It's good for him to feel the triumphs of poor people surviving and making good, achieving the small securities and decencies and seeing their three surviving children do even better. It's good for him also to feel the losses: the old mother in Sweden who never saw her emigrant child again, the fourth child who died young in the farmhouse on the first farm. The history books can tell him who won the Dempsey-Tunney fight but not that his great-grandmother bet a nickel on the outcome; the history books can tell him about the drought years of the 1930s but cannot bring him his great-grandmother's voice as she swept the piled-up field dust from the doorstep and muttered in Swedish, "Dry as ashes." Only his grandmother can tell him those things.

LONG PRAIRIE LEADER

Elsie

January 31, 1983

Elsie Rylander Larson died January 17. She was in her own bedroom, with a bird feeder outside the window and pots of African violets on the dresser. At her bedside were her husband, one of her daughters, and one of her grandchildren. She was my mother-in-law, my neighbor, and my dear friend.

I've written about her often before, of course, but it seems strange to write about her under her own name. It used to be one of her jokes that I couldn't write my column without her various adventures. But while she was the kind of person who engages the world and has adventures, she was also a person who liked her privacy. So I referred to her as "my friend" and "my neighbor up on the hill."

Once, I remember, she accepted more cucumbers than she needed from two or three donors, including me—people with a glut of cucumbers to whom she had mentioned that she wanted to make some pickles. The two of us wound up making dill pickles in quantity on a hot, sticky August night, giggling together over the pot, our eyes prickling with the smell of brine in the room. "I'm sure you'll put this in a column," she said. "And you should because it will make a funny column, but don't you tell anybody my name." I dutifully wrote up the great cucumber caper, referring to "my friend Mrs. X." Nevertheless, her friends greeted her at church by saying, "Well, Elsie, I see your daughter-in-law wrote about you in her column."

That I should treat my mother-in-law with respect and eventually with love was inevitable. She was a loving, generous, warm woman. But that we should become friends was not inevitable at all. She was a small-town Minnesotan, and I was a California poet. Her friends wore suits and haircuts; mine wore jeans and beards. Our political ideas, the ways in which we expressed our religious feelings, many of our tastes could not have been more different.

And yet we did become friends. In part because her generosity of spirit had a way of pushing through barriers and leaping over walls. In part because I was the wife of her son, the mother of three of her grandchildren. But most importantly, it was because she loved nature in all its manifestations. When she became my neighbor on the shores of Big Swan Lake, she shared that love with me.

So we would walk together in the spring woods, and she was always quicker than I was to spot the early spring flowers— hepatica, bloodroot, trillium, violet, wood anemone—flowers whose names she taught me. As the soil warmed, we compared notes on what we were planting, and she gave me slips and transplants. My daisies and chrysanthemums and irises came first from her garden. In midsummer we shared the friendly competition of gardeners, for first, for biggest, for most abundant. In fall we watched together for the passage of the swans, for the pair of bald eagles who spent a day or two by Swan Lake several falls, for the south-flying geese. During her last illness, she asked, over and over, if we had seen geese on the lake. This year the geese migrated high, and though I heard a couple of flocks, I never saw one land. But she saw some swans on the Mississippi one day last fall. It gives me pleasure to remember that, now that she is gone.

Now that I have begun talking about the woman I called Mother, I find it hard to stop. I think of the morning I was mooching around the house at 10:00 a.m., still in slippers and bathrobe. The phone rang. It was Elsie. "Edie, come up," she cried, in a voice full of delight, "I've got purple finches at my feeder!" I threw on my jeans and ran up the hill. There they were, beautiful birds the color of raspberry sherbet. We sat over coffee (some of our happiest times were over coffee) and gloated together on their beauty.

She was a woman with a great zest for life. She liked to meet people, to entertain people, to feed people amply and well. "Nobody ever goes home hungry from Grandma's house," my kids would say. She loved traveling. Up until her final illness she approached life with sometimes startling enthusiasm. A few years back, I remember, she astonished us by going to a demolition derby. One of her students was driving in it, she said; and besides, she just wanted to see what one was like. She was a great lover of games of all kinds, especially Scrabble, at which she beat me roundly every single time we ever played. I used to tell her that if they ever instituted Scrabble-playing as a money sport at Vegas I would back her against the house. She didn't approve of gambling, but I think that amused her.

She had a lively sense of humor but no malice. She liked to talk about her neighbors and friends, but she had no taste for scandal. She had a storehouse of old sayings, some in Swedish and some translated, which I suppose I will be hearing in certain situations the rest of my life. Of politicians: "They offer you gold in green trees." Of a stretch of winding road: "A snake would break its back on that road." And whenever I brought her news of some notable accomplishment, some academic or athletic feat by her grandchildren, she would give me a little pat on the hand and say, "Well, the acorn doesn't fall too far from the tree."

As we were going to her funeral, I noticed a young relative at that peach-fuzz stage of beard growth where the prized potential mustache is barely distinguishable from a smudge of dirt, and I found myself between laughing and weeping. I knew exactly what Elsie would have said: "Put a little cream on it and the cat will lick it off."

Her hands in her coffin were very clean, very folded, very still. They were finished with blowing the noses of small students and grandchildren, with peeling potatoes and stirring gravy, with wrapping presents and spreading bird seed and planting beans and picking spent African violets from the plant. But her brave and joyous spirit lives on, resonating in our hearts like the windy cry of geese flying north.

MORRISON COUNTY RECORD

Gold Hill

December 1, 1991

What somebody from the Midwest sees (what I'm sure John sees) is the barrenness of the landscape. These steep hills are yellowish grey, grey-white, grey. The low, humpy tufts of sagebrush and rabbit brush are more grey than green.

It was not barren to me when I was a child. It was simply The World, the place I saw when I looked through the windows of my house. The bare, gravelly clay was my front yard. The ruinous foundation across the road (not much more ruinous now than it was then) and the fenced-off mine shafts were my playground.

All of western Nevada, in the rain shadow of the Sierras, is semi-desert, its plant communities widely spaced, its vegetation adapted to conserving moisture. But this twisting strip of canyon that winds north from Carson City through Silver City, Gold Hill, and Virginia City is barren in a different way from the sagebrush flats in the basins and the piñon forest on the ranges between them. This is barren because it was stripped of its trees, dug up, dug over, back in the days when it was called Gold Canyon. Those lighter patches of soil polka-dotting every hillside are tailings dumps.

These towns ride the Comstock Lode, an incredible fissure of silver ore that once supported populations as large as 75,000 in

Virginia City, 10,000 across the divide in Gold Hill. There were around 240 people, my mother says, when she lived here in the thirties. The sign at the entrance to town says there are forty now.

I knew in a fuzzy way when I was a kid that we lived on something called the Comstock Lode, that my father worked at the Crown Point (first in the "breaking house," then as a hard-rock miner, finally in the mill) and that the mine produced silver.

On this bright October day, we drive up this steep grade again. Everything looks somehow familiar, but nothing looks specific. It's my mother who finds the house across the road and a little uphill from the long-closed building that says "Crown Point Mill."

I am surprised the house is still there. My childhood memories are of a tall narrow building, three rooms (one of them tiny) downstairs, three rooms up. So tall and tottery-looking a house that my dad installed a couple of telegraph poles as props. The exterior walls were weathered brown. I don't know whether they had ever been painted. My parents moved there in 1937, renting the place for fifteen dollars a month and glad to have it.

And I do not know if I would have recognized this place without my mother's help. The narrow central section has had extensions added to front and rear, a wide porch built on the side where the main door opens. There are casings around the windows. Those French doors opening onto the porch are new. And the roof—

But the woodshed is Dad's woodshed. I remember him, a good-looking fellow with a dashing Clark Gable mustache, splitting pine. In his early twenties.

A sign in what used to be my grandmother's garden, a sign rusty and hard to read but still more recent than my tenancy in this place, says, "Gold Hill Brewery. This slender residence was the eastern one half of the old brewery." Other words trail off into rust, but these are sufficient to cause my mother, who was a total abstainer when she lived here, to puff up like a startled cat. "Well," she says in a voice full of suspicion and outrage, "it may have been a brewery, but for six years it was my home!"

I open the French doors. Good heavens! Victorian furniture! In my mind's eye I remember the big kitchen wood range, the yellow-calcimined kitchen walls, the isinglass window in the front of the little parlor stove.

It was my house then, but we left in 1942 when I was seven, and John is pointing out "no trespassing" signs to me.

Across the road, in the Gold Hill Hotel and Saloon (incorporating an old brick building that was Louis' Bar, back then) a fellow in a big Stetson with big hair, big beard, grizzly bear slide on his neckerchief, big belt over substantial belly, and a decorative dagger in his boot informs us that this one-time brewery, one-time near-shack now rents in its transmogrified state for 150 dollars a night.

We poke around a little more, take a few pictures, drive on.

This place has as bloody, bizarre, and tumultuous a history as can be imagined. Prospectors, politicians, bankers, Indians, unionists, secessionists all struggled for survival and wealth. Great fortunes were made here, and some fortunes were lost. There were fires underground and above it. Mark Twain wrote for the newspaper.

This history, the tourists' history, is fascinating, and I'm glad I'm learning it.

But it's not why I came here.

MORRISON COUNTY RECORD

A Bell for Santa

December 22, 1991

When I was in Gold Hill with my mother, we drove up the grade to Virginia City.

Virginia City is, as they say in the tourist brochures, a picturesque western mining town where the rip-roaring days of the Comstock Lode are preserved. Tour buses arrive in Virginia City frequently, disgorging hordes of tourists to stroll the plank sidewalks and patronize the old saloons, like the Bucket of Blood, and the new tourist establishments in the old buildings.

When we lived in Gold Hill, my father worked at the Crown Point Mine, and active mining still went on up the grade in Virginia City. Both places were gritty, working towns full of old mine shafts and unpainted, collapsing buildings. But people lived there, people who celebrated Christmas.

Every Christmas we went up that steep grade to the Lions Club Christmas party. Every known child in both towns was invited and called up personally to receive a present. I only remember one of those presents, one which pleased me and mortified my parents. Whoever had matched Lions' gifts to recipients had mistaken my gender, and, as a result, little Edie Alcock received a wind-up tank.

I enjoyed sending my little tank creeping across the living

60

room floor. When I put a book on the floor, the tank could laboriously creep up over the top of it and down the other side. I don't think I ever realized that my tank was a small replica of a war wagon at that time killing people wholesale across the sea.

My sister, Joy, was less fortunate. For three years in a row, she got the same gift—a little toy broom. By the time she received her third broom, she knew perfectly well from the shape of the package what present she was getting. She had a hard time forcing a smile.

Christmas in Virginia City also involved the church pageant. I am sure I was in such performances, but apart from blurred memories of Christmas carols and a lit tree in church, memories that could have come from later pageants, I mostly remember things Joy did, and those mostly because my mother has never stopped talking about them.

Joy was my only sibling, two and one-half years younger than I. We were very close. I was the thoughtful, shy one. I was nearsighted too (though nobody had recognized it yet), which made me clumsy. Joy was a bold little thing, talkative, unafraid, and cheerful. When we were "playing Indian" I decided a proper Indian camp needed a campfire; Joy stole the kitchen matches. That time the Virginia City Fire Department came screaming down the grade to put out the blazing sagebrush.

My mother would know how old Joy was when, as part of the Christmas program, she was called on to recite a comic poem called "The Moo-Cow Moo." I know she was small enough that the first lines, "I guess you think I am too small/To stand up here and speak at all," came out, "I guess you think I am too 'mall/To 'tand up here and 'peak a-tall."

The only other thing I remember about that poem is the immortal quatrain that runs:

The Moo-Cow Moo has lots of fun
Just swinging her tail about.
But when she opens her mouth, I run,
'Cause that's where the moo comes out!

Joy's recitation was a roaring success. Numerous people told me how cute my little sister was. No wonder I don't remember what I did in that program!

I suppose the ultimate in cuteness—or sweetness, or niceness—came when Santa was distributing gifts at church. Joy had somewhere gotten a little bell. As Santa was finishing his task, she ran up to him quite spontaneously, held up her bell and said, "Here, Santa, here's someping for 'oo."

At least, that's the way Mom has always told the story.

You would think the foundation for sibling rivalry of a vicious kind might have been laid then and there. There were times when Joy and I had our differences, our jealousies, our fights. But she has been dead since 1959. I envy people who have sisters with whom they can fight.

Charles Dickens' immortal *A Christmas Carol* is a ghost story. Christmas is full of images of new life, its centerpiece always the Babe in the manger. But I'm sure I am not the only person who remembers the dead with special poignancy on Christmas.

At Christmas we are all supposed to love our families with special intensity, and mostly we do. But out of wanting everything to be perfect, spending too much, and working too hard, we can sometimes get so mad at our near and dear that we wouldn't mind shoving them up the chimney!

The lesson Ebenezer Scrooge learns in *A Christmas Carol* is that the "humbug" of Christmas is more important, in the long run, than a fat bank balance and the solitary person's absolute right to be as nasty, stingy, and bad-tempered as he pleases. After a decade that glorified deal-makers like Michael Milken and Donald Trump, Dickens' old-fashioned message has not lost its point.

It really was sweet and generous for a little girl to want to give something back to Santa. Sweetness and generosity and memories mellowed by time are what Christmas is about.

I wish them to all my readers. May the memories built this season all be sweet and generous ones.

MORRISON COUNTY RECORD

That Edie

April 30, 1990

If my dear namesake grandmother is watching me from the
next world—which may well be what she expected to do—she
must be quite astounded. Especially during gardening season.

She was the first gardener I ever knew. If she could see me
now, thumbing through seed catalogues, poking seeds into dirt,
hovering over little pots with a squeeze bottle, she would not believe it. Where is the day-dreaming child whose one and only
attempt at voluntary weeding was such a catastrophy? Is it really
"that Edie" down on her knees in the dirt?

My paternal grandmother, Edith Eleanor Rigsby Alcock, spent
a lot of time down on her knees in the dirt, especially during World
War II when her garden took on heroic dimensions. Gardens
then were Victory Gardens, especially hers.

I don't think Grandma had many victories in her life. She
had fought for the chance to take nurse's training, which her
family had thought an unsuitable activity for a Canadian lady of
good family in 1903. Then she had had one of those hopeless
Victorian affairs of the heart with a man who could not marry her.

The man she did marry was a full generation older than she
and had a large family from an earlier marriage. His health was
poor, and he found it hard to get and hold jobs. They were always
moving.

By the time I got to know her, Grandma was a widow, a stout woman in her sixties, her gray hair wound up in a small bun. I was the first child of a marriage that had caused her great anguish, not only because my parents were nineteen and sixteen and had only known each other six weeks when they married, not only because it was the middle of the Depression and my father had no job, but because she felt Charlie had married "beneath himself." (Yes, she really did talk like that.) In due time she came to value and to love my mother, and told her as much—on her deathbed. Not till then.

It must have been a grim life for Grandma, the live-in mother-in-law, even if the first baby was named after her. No money, no elegance, no status. And Hitler bombing London. As a transplanted Canadian, a subject of the king, she felt every bomb.

Then the bombs fell on Pearl Harbor, and the United States entered the war, and my parents both went to work in a defense plant. Suddenly, she was not just a mother-in-law. She was someone freeing a worker for the war effort, helping to beat the Nazis. And the garden, which quickly filled almost the entire backyard behind the two-bedroom California bungalow, was a Victory Garden. Every radish, every squash, every carrot was aimed directly at Hitler.

Maybe I made her life tough because I resented my mother's absence, but I really doubt that. I think I made her life tough because it is the nature of children to get away with what they can. I got out of weeding the garden or practicing the piano whenever I could. Then I would hear her talking to my parents about "that Edie."

I don't remember what I had done, or not done, the time she went after me with a lath, her usual paddle, to administer the usual spanking. I remember running away, dodging around the room. And I realized that she was not going to catch me. She was a fat old lady with a bad heart. She was also the lady who had read me all those fairy tales. It was mean of me to make her chase me like that.

That was a shock. I wanted my namesake to be powerful. I didn't want her to be a person who could be outwitted and outrun by an eight-year-old child. Something had changed in our relationship and would never be the same again.

On this occasion, I decided to do something nice for her, without even being asked. She spent a lot of time weeding. (It never occurred to me, then, that perhaps she enjoyed it. I had to become a gardener myself before I learned that.) There was a row of something—I knew not what—but something planted, a row all full of coarse, larger plants. I would weed it for Grandma.

It was one of the best-intentioned acts of my life. Unfortunately, my botany was shaky. I left a neat row of wild mustard from which I had carefully obliterated every trace of Grandma's stock.

That Edie, at it again!

I often feel she is with me when I weed. She might not approve of everything I have done with my life, but I think she would like my garden.

MORRISON COUNTY RECORD

Good-bye, Miss Piggy

October 1980

Miss Piggy came to live with us on April 18, 1978. Miss Piggy was a spotted Duroc-cross sow. Back in 1978 she weighed around forty pounds. Eric bought her as a feeder pig; in other words, we intended to ship her out at the end of the summer and get her back as pork chops.

She turned out to be an animal of sparkling personality and ingratiating habits. The use of words like "sparkling" and "ingratiating" to refer to a pig may surprise some readers, for pigs are widely misunderstood. If Eric were writing this column instead of me, he would now spend a thousand well-chosen words clearing up those misunderstandings. He would write at length about porcine intelligence, about the fact that pigs (unlike people) do not eat more than they need, about the fact that pigs have no sweat glands, and so, in hot weather, they must wallow to keep cool, so wallowing is no sign of a love of filth. He would come in with his clinching argument that a pig always chooses a "bathroom" space in its pen so that it does not foul its sleeping or eating area. And Eric would give all his readers a solid scolding for their habit of using the word "pig" as an insult, in expressions such as "eat like a pig."

But even among those noble beasts the swine, some have

more personality than others. Miss Piggy had personality. She made it clear that she liked people and enjoyed their company. She would put her trotters up on the rail and beg us to scratch behind her ears. In her svelte youth she would celebrate our attentions by racing around the pen, kicking up her heels. She was, pardon the expression, a ham.

Come fall, Eric said, "Do you suppose we could get her bred and keep her?" We decided we could.

She gave us four excellent litters and always appreciated company when she was farrowing. A new litter of pigs became a biannual drama in the barn. On frosty winter days when I went out to dispense feed and water, she grunted sociably. She was company.

She also got bigger every year. Unlike most animals, a pig does not reach adult size and stop growing. By late summer 1980, she was well over 600 pounds. Eric had said a number of times, "I'm never going to ship Miss Piggy out; when she dies I'll have her taxidermied and put her in my room." But he was beginning to realize that so huge an animal would leave no room for Eric. He was beginning to say, "Maybe I'll just have her head stuffed to remember her by."

Then she was due for her fourth litter, and she was in trouble. What had come naturally to her before seemed to be not just labor, but difficult and exacting labor. "You're lucky it's not hot," the vet said after he looked her over. "If the temperature was up in the eighties or nineties, this would kill her."

Finally the litter arrived, as healthy and vigorous as usual. But for a day or two after farrowing, Miss Piggy would simply drop where she was and lie there. She had to be shoved and kicked into position to nurse. She was exhausted. It was clear that this litter of pigs had taken a lot out of her. Another would kill her. She was just not going to be a usable brood sow anymore.

What to do with a 650-pound sow who couldn't have any more little pigs? All by herself she took up a lot of room. She ate plenty. We couldn't really afford, as in Eric's early fantasy, to keep her for the rest of her natural life. If we were going to continue raising pigs, we needed to put that space and that food and that work at the other end of the manure shovel into a younger, productive sow.

So we came down to that hard choice farmers have to make, the one that ends with the chopping block or the truck from the locker plant. It was the part of farming nobody liked, but it was unescapably part of an occupation in which the squirmy, squeally little pig from which we strip his birth membranes, the wobbly-legged calf we help bring into the light of the barn, is also our meal ticket. "It doesn't do to get attached to them," farmers say. But they do get attached to them. Especially to the beasts like Miss Piggy, who are friendly and smart and like humans.

I have friends who are vegetarians. To them the relationship that begins with husbandry and ends with the locker plant truck is cruel and unnatural. They don't want their diet to be based on killing. Unfortunately all organisms live off other organisms. We cannot raise anything without competing with other living organisms for the use of that particular parcel of food energy that winds up on our table. Bugs, weeds, birds, gophers, rats, mice, and rabbits all compete for a place at the human table. At some point, with cultivator or poison or trap or gun, we have to eliminate at least enough of those competitors to make a crop. To me, it does not make much difference whether I eat an animal killed directly or a carrot defended with poison, trap, or gun. For the time being, I eat the energy I need. In due time my body will lend that energy to other organisms.

So, when the little pigs were weaned, the locker plant truck came around, and John and I shook the corn in the pan and led our old friend up the ramp into the truck for her last trip. And then Eric bought a nice little gilt he had his eye on. The cycle began again.

ST. CLOUD TIMES

The Show Must Go On

December 9, 1981

Eric went off to school this morning singing a Christmas song. The choir is getting ready for the Christmas program. I hope the program is a success and exciting, but I hope it is not exciting like the Christmas program my sophomore year at Fremont High. That was the year one of the tenors threw up all over the first sopranos during the second verse of "Silent Night." As I remember, during the first afternoon presentation—indeed, as we were singing "Shepherds quake at the sight"—old Ronnie cut loose in the third row. They hustled Ronnie out, but his memory lingered. I was a second soprano and, therefore, somewhat outside the main line of fire. It was not fun for any of us, but it must have been purely awful for the girls in the second row. "The show must go on" took on a new poignancy (or pungency) to me at that point.

I can remember a couple of "show-must-go-on" episodes involving the Grade School Public Schools Week presentation in Sunnyvale, too. As with Christmas pageants, Public Schools Week pageants were fixed in content, and for several years the pageant was called something like "Our Friends Around the World." This meant an Irish song, a Dutch dance, an Italian song, a Russian dance—well, you get the idea. When I was in seventh grade one of the dance numbers was a lively Russian affair called the Kurobishka. (I've never seen the word written out—that's how we pronounced it.) It involved a lot of fast spinning and partner-changing. The girls wore full skirts, and the boys wore belted blouses and baggy, Cossack-type pants. At the last rehearsal the folk dance teacher had a few sharp words to say to the male Kurobishka dancers. "None of this business of hauling on your dance costume over your regular clothes," she said. "It looks bulky and clumsy and it's not authentic! I don't want to see anybody tonight with anything on under their costumes but underwear."

So of course, on one of those fast spins, one of the male dancers suffered an elastic failure at the waistband, and his Cossack pants came whooshing down around his Cossack boots on the stage of the Sunnyvale civic auditorium in front of three hundred people. Fortunately he had not taken the teacher at her word and was wearing something more than underwear. He behaved with marvelous adaptive quickness, whipping up his collapsing pantaloons and whizzing off into the wings all in one move. He left his partner spinning and clapping alone, but a fellow can't think of everything.

Even greater presence of mind was shown by one of the boys playing a missionary priest in the Public Schools Week program my eighth-grade year. That was 1949, and we did a California history pageant to commemorate the gold rush centennial. The second scene was of a tranquil mission garden in which a couple of Spanish padres in their long cassocks stood benevolently around, supervising the labors of some presumably happy Indians. Behind them was a really impressive piece of scenery: the side and bell-tower of a Spanish mission. The curtain opened, the off-stage narrator said half a sentence, and then, to a great "Ooooo" from the audience, the whole mission flat, tower and all, came tipping over onto the stage. One of the student padres lifted a protecting hand and just stood there, supporting the flat, till the curtain closed. It was a great and even appropriate piece of theater— just not in the script.

My final memories of non-scripted dramatic movements revolve around the senior class play at Fremont High. I had been cast as a middle-aged lady, and, in the interests of greying my hair, the make-up crew gobbed it up with white shoe polish. It looked and felt like string for some time afterwards.

But that mishap was nothing to what happened to one of the boys, a kid I'll call Ken Jones. That was not his name, but he would no doubt just as soon forget his role in the one-act allegorical play called "Slave with Two Faces." Ken was cast as Life—which gives some notion of the kind of play it was—and, like the other actors, he was dressed in sort of medieval clothing: long, full skirts and laced bodices for the girls and, for Ken, trunk hose, a snug doublet, and a sweeping cape. His first entrance involved a dramatic leap onto the stage.

What nobody—not the actors or the faculty director or the costume crew—seemed to have realized was that a high school kid known to most of the audience, leaping onto a stage in trunk hose, tight doublet, and cape, even in costume colors of mustard yellow and moss green, would not look like Life. He would look like Kenny Jones playing Superman. Throughout the two afternoon performances for the student body the poor guy had to leap onto the stage and whip his cape around to a continuous cascade of high school buddies' belly laughs. I wonder that he didn't run off stage, grab his pants and shoes and join the Army right then and there.

But he stuck it out—he and the rest of the cast—conscientiously reading serious, allegorical lines to an audience that was rolling in the aisles.

The evening performance was all right, though. The evening audience was parents, and parents don't laugh unless the playbill says, "A comedy." Sometimes a student performer can do with a few parents in the audience.

LONG PRAIRIE LEADER

Blood in the Kitchen

November 26, 1984

The god of ancient Greek drama was Dionysos, the god of the vine. As one would expect of a wine god, Dionysos liked a good laugh, which is why Greek culture produced both tragedies and comedies. Dionysos might have found it both natural and diverting when, in the interest of promoting the dramatic arts, I recently found myself racing down a frozen driveway—fifteen-degree air slithering up bare legs, bathrobe and hair flying in the wind— screaming, "Eric! Eric!" and waving a bottle of red food coloring.

But this drama really begins with Eric's fake blood. Eric, the resident kid, bought a tube of fake blood three years ago, when he was a callow youth of fourteen. The stuff in question is a gelatin-like substance that can be blopped or dabbled on the skin. He would swagger into the house and drop into a chair, causing his mother or another concerned person to exclaim, "Eric! Are you all right?" Of course this only worked once or twice per person, after which he would be greeted merely with, "Into the fake blood again, eh?"

I hadn't seen the fake blood for a long time. Then bright and early one morning, about ten minutes before the school bus was due, Eric rushed into the kitchen exclaiming, "Mom, where's my blood?"

It took a minute to figure out that he was looking for his fake blood. It took a couple of minutes more to establish that he needed the fake blood for his role in a musical called *Calamity Jane.* As Lieutenant Danny Gilmartin, recent survivor of an Indian attack, he was to reel into a frontier watering hole, the Golden Garter, there to be bandaged and consoled by Calamity. The first public performance of this dramatic vehicle was scheduled to take place that very day. And Lt. Gilmartin, played by my kid Eric, whose bus was due in ten minutes, needed some blood for the occasion.

After the usual maternal comments, which ran along the lines of, "Why didn't you tell me about this sooner?" and "Why is it my responsibility to keep track of your fake blood?" I joined in a search. Five minutes passed. I was certain the missing gore was not upstairs. He was equally sure it wasn't downstairs. "I had it out in the truck," he said, "but it's not there."

We were within three minutes of bus time. "Suppose I got some red food coloring," Eric said, "and mixed it up with vaseline, would that work?"

"Well, it might," I said, "but you'd have to be careful. It might stain clothes and things."

This, as the bus roared off toward the school.

"Well, gimme your food coloring then. I guess I'll have to take the pickup."

I spent several minutes rummaging, and finally, triumphantly, I came up with the right shape bottle, which I handed to my son.

"Mo-om!" he cried. (You know that sound kids make when they're truly frustrated, the sound between a hungry lamb and a steer in distress.) "Mo-om, this is *blue* food coloring!"

I felt tempted to suggest, since even using the truck he was going to cut things fine, that he write a line into the play about Lt. Gilmartin being a blue-blooded aristocrat. But I went on with my motherly duty, rummaging shelves and cupboards with increasing desperation.

"I've gotta leave, I'll be late otherwise."

"Will you have time to buy some food coloring before school?" I hollered after him, but he was out the door. As I stood there in the silence that follows a big dramatic scene, I saw an amazing sight. Directly in front of me, where I must have looked at it and around it a dozen times, was a bottle of red food coloring.

I've already described my frantic rush into the yard, made more frantic by the fact that Eric was already into the truck and in motion. At the last possible moment before he took off down the driveway, I managed by wild shouting and arm-waving to catch his eye. He took the food coloring and pulled out of the yard.

I pinned up my hair and cinched up my bathrobe and walked at a somewhat more dignified pace toward the house, grateful that I didn't live in town, where my contribution to the dramatic arts might have enlivened my neighbors' morning coffee.

Needless to say, Lt. Gilmartin staggered into the Golden Garter with bloody convincingness for the run of the play, and, after the last performance, my bottle of red food coloring was returned to me. It was dry as a bone. I only complained mildly. All of us need to make occasional contributions to the arts.

MORRISON COUNTY RECORD

The Last Time

May 13, 1985

It was just like all the other times. Rush through the dishes. Wash off the day's dust. Put on some clothes fancier than garden grubbies. Drive into town. This time the trees are in half-leaf, the fields green with May, though we've driven often enough past bare trees and snow or the blazing colors of fall.

Park in the school lot, walk in past the lunchroom doors, into the auditorium, which is also a gym, with curtained stage on one side, basketball hoops at both ends. Smile and nod to friends. We seat ourselves in folding chairs. When the choir begins singing "Simple Gifts," I pick out the voice of my last child.

Let's see, the first time I went to a school program because a child of mine was singing was back in the fall of 1964. Good heavens, that's twenty-one years ago. The blue-eyed kid who stood up on that stage, earnestly singing "Oh, Christmas Tree" while absent-mindedly rolling his shirt up and down over his tummy, is celebrating his twenty-sixth birthday next week. He was five then. So the math is right.

The only trouble is, I feel not much older than when I sang "Gianniana Mia" with the seventh-grade choir.

This will be the last school program where our child is making music that we'll see.

Kids do grow up and go. Nothing wrong with that. When my son now edging twenty-six was six, he loved a book about a family of birds. One of the nestlings, Allen, would not try to fly, but just sat in the nest getting bigger and fatter while poor old Mama and Papa wore their wings out fetching him succulent worms. A sneaky cat with a taste for fat nestlings finally frightened Allen out of his cozy nest and into life on his own.

Dan and I would laugh over the last page together, where Mama and Papa Bird flew along smiling with Allen flying between them. "Fat Al was out of the nest at last," Dan would read triumphantly, proud of his literacy, approving of the moral.

And truth to tell, my two offspring who are gone keep in pretty good touch. They write. They call. Now and then they ask our advice. Sometimes they even take it. It was not always thus.

When the music I hear is "Pomp and Circumstance" and the last kid walks down the aisle in his graduation robe, as he will in a couple of weeks, I will drop a few tears. But the end of one phase in life is the beginning of another.

Twenty-one years of school programs. But the memories go back beyond that, to Sunday School pageants and Public Schools Week programs and piano recitals. Reciting "I Wandered Lonely as a Cloud" at age six in a one-room school in Gold Hill, Nevada. My sister (who died when my oldest kid was three months), singing "Stout Hearted Men" at the age of eleven. The wonderful look of concentration my daughter always wore when she played the saxophone.

A few years ago Mother Rylander sat next to me, watching programs like this. How many years her memories must have gone back, to her own childhood, to programs in which her children took part, to programs in which her students participated. How she loved this time of year. How she'd love to see the last kid graduate. But she's out of the nest and gone.

The kid singing now is the motor-head, the one fascinated with taking things apart and seeing how they work. My father was like that. He once entirely rebuilt a two-place airplane in our single-car attached garage. We recovered the wings in the living room. One wing would just fit corner to corner. I could share Dad's enthusiasms for singing and literature and flying, but not for engines. He and the kid would have had a great time talking airplanes. But he died when the kid was three. Life is full of missed connections.

The harmonies of the music are imperfect. The kid admits later that he came in at the wrong point on "This Land Is Your

Land." But we aren't here as music critics, and even performed by amateurs whose young minds will wander to Saturday night or the girl in the next row, music harmonizes the missed connections. Men who are bones in foreign tombs reach out to us, saying, "Listen. Pay attention." The beauty of the utterance sets us free to weep the tears that do not burn but heal.

Last week the air smelled of willow pollen. I notice as we walk out to the car that it smells now of wild plum blossoms.

MORRISON COUNTY RECORD

Small-Town Class of 1985
Goes Out into the World

June 1985

The first cars and trucks start coming into town about 7:00, the ones with glass packs and fake fur and pin striping, with rock station stickers and little chains made of pull tabs from cans draped above the front windows. They come into this town that is like so many others, past the working stores and the stores with blank, dirty windows. They park behind the school that serves kindergarten through grade twelve.

Later the others come, the newer pickups and the family sedans with the bumper stickers that say "Farming is Your Bread and Butter." It's a warm, bright evening that carries smells a long way, and the cars have driven through swaths of odor. Last lilacs. Crushed alfalfa. Ripe, suffocating richness past a field where someone has pumped out his liquid manure.

There is reserved seating for families, and each mother is given a rose. Still there is plenty of room, both reserved and unreserved, in the gym/auditorium. The school band sits on one side. Up on stage the chairs wait. In glittery, silver letters the class motto hangs above the stage. It says they will make their own paths. It says they will lead the way.

The band begins to play Elgar. The erect figures in the silver-grey robes march in slowly. When there are fewer than thirty in

78

the graduating class, one playing of "Pomp and Circumstance" accompanies everybody on stage nicely. Under the mortarboards, their hair shines like silk. Skirts of new dresses in pastel colors ruffle around the girls' knees. Half the boys are wearing ties. All over Minnesota, all over America, students are marching onto stages and up into bleachers tonight.

Except for the people on stage and the people in the audience, it is just like every other commencement. For them, it is like no other in the history of the world. There are kids here with their college plans made and scholarship money in their pockets. There are others for whose families this night represents an achievement, a first.

And there are those who didn't make it this far. Some are sitting in the audience. Some are married. Some have children. Some already have tastes and habits that will do them no good in the world of work into which they've launched themselves half-prepared.

The principal does not mention the ones who didn't make it this far, though no doubt he thinks about them. But he presents the members of the class of 1985 to their parents and friends. The young pastor gives an invocation. The band plays. The chorus sings songs about eagles and mountains and rivers.

Instead of hiring some local dignitary to tell the graduates that the future is before them, this school has students give brief commencement addresses. The class president, representatives of senior boys and senior girls, the salutatorian and the valedictorian each stand their few moments behind the podium, speaking their pieces.

Mostly what they say is, I've spent thirteen years of my life with the same people, and it wasn't always easy, but I learned a lot. I grew up in this town where everybody knows his third cousin and goes to his wedding, when anytime I want I can go out to Grandpa's farm and help him with the cows or hunt squirrels in the woodlot or take the old boat out onto the lake and catch a few sunnies. This is the world in which I grew up, and it's pretty small. To tell the truth, the big world I see on TV is kind of scary. But I'm grown and educated now, and I know I have to leave, so good-bye and thanks.

The three short rows rise one at a time; the names are called, and they all step forward. The pretty and less pretty, the bright and less bright, the letter club members and the cheerleaders and the kids with awards in music and drama, the guy who can make an engine do anything, and the class clown. And the piece of paper for which they've put in thirteen years, the one with the slightly idealized line drawing of the school, is put into their hands.

They march back and solemnly, all at once, transfer the tassels on their mortarboards from one side to the other. And the audience, the brothers and sisters and grandparents and parents and friends, wipe away a few tears and clap like crazy.

The pastor gives the benediction. The band plays. The graduates stride out, the flashbulbs snap, hands are shaken and faces kissed. The cake with the picture of the diploma on it is set on the table. The wet towels come off the trays of little sandwiches. The kegs are tapped.

The class of 1985 goes out into the world.

ST. CLOUD TIMES

Good-bye to the
Growl and Whine

September 1, 1986

It's strange the way a single sound can summon up an era in life. For years, the sound that governed my day more than any other was the engine growl and transmission whine of the school bus that stopped at the end of our driveway around 7:45 a.m. The bus engine signalled the terminal phase of The Mad Rush. If the growl and whine sounded while Dan or Shireen or Eric was still in the bathroom, we had trouble.

The early morning, from waking up through cooking breakfast to last minute panics ("I don't have any clean socks!"), announcements ("I wrote you down for bars for the band thing tonight, Mom."), and counter panics ("What kind of bars? What band thing? Tonight?!?"), was dominated by getting the kids off to school. After the final gear-grinding departure, the house always seemed incredibly quiet. There was always plenty of work to do, but it didn't come at me in an explosive forty-five minute burst of decision making, at an hour when deciding between oatmeal and eggs for breakfast was hard work. And it didn't include outcries of, "Why can't I go? Everyone else is going? I'll be the only kid in my class who hasn't gone!"

The growl and whine would enter my life again around 3:45, followed quickly by a banging of doors. The Great Return was taking place. ("Hi, Mom, what's there to eat?") It meant I got up from the typewriter at which, if my life was in some reasonable order, I had been sitting since 1:00 p.m., committing literature, and started dinner. Even if I didn't really need to start dinner that soon, between loud voices and the thump of the refrigerator opening and shutting and rock-and-roll cranked downstairs and the television set blasting out cartoons or Hogan's Heroes reruns upstairs, literature became difficult after The Great Return.

This week the growl and whine will start again, signalling a new school year. In fact, the bus still stops at the end of my driveway to pick up and drop off the kids who live down the road. But I notice it only in passing. In other people's houses, The Mad Rush is taking place. Not in mine, not anymore.

A television commercial of some years ago showed a little kid getting on the school bus the first time, his hand sliding slowly, reluctantly out of Mama's. That commercial always made me blink and blow my nose, even though I knew perfectly well that the advertiser was only trying to sell me life insurance. Yet I can watch without the least bit of a tear as the bus takes off, totally devoid of Rylander kids.

There are no more explosions at breakfast, no more demands for bars or socks, no more frantic, last-minute dashes into twenty-below mornings by everyday-shampooing, wet-headed teenagers too cool to wear hats. ("It'll mash my hair down!") There are no hollers, slams, or feeding frenzies at 3:45. If I want to finish the page I'm working on, neither Tweety Bird nor Colonel Klink nor Motley Crue roaring "Bang Your Head" will come between me and my muse.

Is it quiet around here? Is there less excitement? Sure. Do I miss all that?

Are you kidding?

I wouldn't have missed having kids for the world. Not everybody is cut out for the work of raising a complete human being from scratch, with all the touching and funny moments—and all the terrors—that parenthood entails. Raising kids is hard work, a tougher job than anybody who hasn't tried it can imagine, harder and more important work than Americans as a country seem willing to admit. A senator in Washington recently said that it didn't matter what kind of childcare kids had under the age of three, assuming they were safe and all, because kids don't learn anything till they're three. Anybody who's cared for children knows that kids are learning from their first breath outside the womb—learning to trust or not trust, to explore or stay put, to experiment with language or shut up.

Whatever I taught my children, I learned just as much from them. A parent has to be stable (right there when needed) but also flexible (ready, willing, and able to produce clean socks and yummy bars at short notice). Has to have a sense of humor (how could any parent survive without it?) but know when not to laugh. (The heartbreaks of six- or sixteen-year-olds can be pretty funny to adults, but they still hurt at six or sixteen.)

Above all, a parent has to know when to let go. The little kids, even the teary, timid ones, have to get on that bus. And in due time they have to get off that bus and head on out the road into their own lives.

If there's one thing being a parent teaches a person, it's how to say good-bye.

MORRISON COUNTY RECORD

Waiting for the Name

January 6, 1986

It's just about the same temperature and humidity level as when I attended my last graduation. That was in Minnesota in May. This is Florida in December. That time the gowns were silver-grey. There were twenty-four graduates, walking very slowly into a modest-sized gym/auditorium to the strains of a high school band playing Elgar's "Pomp and Circumstance." This time the graduates are so many that their names, in small print, fill up fourteen and one-half pages of program. The gowns are black, the auditorium very large, and Elgar is being played on an organ. But it's still "Pomp and Circumstance," and all the people in the stands are here this warm December day for the same reason all those folks from Grey Eagle and Burtrum were in the Grey Eagle gym last May. We have all come to see somebody dear to us receive a degree.

Here comes the procession, marching onto the auditorium floor while we crane our necks from the bleachers. Here come the marshalls, the dignitaries, the faculty, the degree candidates, all in those flowing gowns, which go back to medieval universities.

Medieval universities were strictly for male clergy, mostly for male clergy from noble families. The notion that ordinary folks needed or deserved higher education (or any education) is pretty new. And less than a hundred years ago, respected educators were arguing that the female brain was too small to bear the rigors of academic study.

A great variety of people have born the rigors of study at this state-supported institution. Glancing at the program, I encounter names like Kassem Ahmad Ibadi, Kin Shing Lee, Perseus Jhabvala, Titus Reji Ninan Kayalakakathu, and Ana Ofelia De Jesus Menenses. Here and there people in the stands grab each others' arms and point. A pretty black girl in the hood of a Master's Degree candidate flashes a sudden grin up to a section of the stands, and fourteen people, all ages from grandparent to babe in arms, give her a personal standing ovation.

Then I'm arm-grabbing myself. "There she is!"

She got up early to press her robe. (She went through high school in army fatigue pants.) Her hair shines under the pertly-cocked mortarboard. My goodness, not only smart and pretty but, to her mother's amazement, organized!

Just as every person receiving a degree today represents the hopes and dreams of other people, so everybody in the stands is here as a sort of representative. I think about this girl's grandmother, who went back to school to get a degree in her fifties. The girl nursed her grandmother the last days of her life. And of my father, a self-educated man who loved learning. And of the girl's father, who is teaching a college class in Minnesota this hour of a December Friday—

Elgar finishes, everyone is seated, the blessings of heaven are invoked and the national anthem sung. The president of the university introduces the commencement speaker. The commencement speaker begins to talk about the responsibility citizens (especially college graduates) have to support and carry on higher education.

Then there is an extraordinary rustling in the bleachers across from us. People are moving around. Arms are waved. A security man crosses the floor quickly. The speaker stops in mid-speech.

Clearly someone has fallen ill, fainted, convulsed or had a coronary. Now there is a whole cluster of people in the bleachers, a couple of them security men. And now two degree candidates, robes, mortarboards and all. Are they children of the sick person, medically trained, or both? There is rushing around on the floor of the auditorium. For a moment the crowd clears, and there in the stands is a remarkable tableau. An older man, in "going to commencement" clothes, is lying back along a bleacher bench. A grey-haired woman leans over him and strokes his forehead. A girl in mortarboard and gown holds his hand, maybe taking his pulse. A boy in mortarboard and gown stands at his feet.

Then one of the security guards brings a wheelchair to the foot of the bleachers. The low buzz of conversation stops as the stricken man is helped to his feet and walked slowly, slowly down to the chair. There is a group intake of breath as they ease him in and a wave of applause as he is wheeled away, sitting upright. Not okay—maybe very ill—but not unconscious, not dead.

The commencement speaker thanks us for our quiet and concern and resumes his address. The ceremony returns to normal. The degrees are awarded. I hope the guy in the wheelchair is close enough and well enough to hear the name he's been waiting for and feel that delight I feel as I hear the name I've been waiting for: ". . . Rita Davis Rosenthal, William R. Rupp, Shireen Ellen Rylander—"

MORRISON COUNTY RECORD

Upata Lake

June 9, 1986

When my daughter, Shireen, was fourteen months old, she was snatched from the comparative sophistication of Monterey Bay, tucked into a car with big brother, Mom, Dad, and the family possessions and hauled from California to Minnesota. She doesn't remember those early years. What she remembers is Upata Lake.

The first year we spent in Minnesota, we held family picnics on Big Swan Lake and finally established ourselves there for good in 1973. Even when nobody was living in it, the lake cottage on Swan was the family gathering place for three generations and several branches. Here on Memorial Day, Fourth of July, and Labor Day, the big folks would talk and eat and fish. The little folks would reacquaint themselves with the tire swing, the woods, the hammock, and the cousins. If it was warm, they'd go swimming. And along the way, they were initiated into the rites of worm digging and bobber watching.

When Shireen was four or five, her father and I were talking about some event that had taken place during one of those family gatherings at Swan Lake. Shireen was outraged, "That lake is not Swan Lake," she said. "That lake is called Upata Lake."

All those years of family stories about things that had happened "up at the lake" had become, for her, the name of the family place: Upata Lake.

Shireen lives near much more notable bodies of water now. A short drive from her house takes a visiting mother to the blue, mild, warm waters of the Atlantic. It's also possible to cruise down the Florida Inter-Coastal Waterway (we did) on a yacht—borrowed, but still a yacht. South Florida is full of beautiful expensive homes, beautiful expensive cars, beautifully dressed, expensive looking men and women. There's not much of that on Upata Lake—just farms, houses, summer cottages, docks, rowboats, and the family john boat with the six-horse motor.

The end of this May, Shireen came back for a visit to the old folks and Upata Lake. Toward the end of her visit we went out fishing one afternoon. As we moved along still-submerged reeds, we could see schools of sunfish darting away. Here and there, the bigger, narrower shape of a bass patrolled his nesting area.

It didn't take long to get bait into the water. It took Shireen a little longer to re-learn skills she hadn't used for four years. She hung bait up in reeds, got line snarled, lost fish. Meanwhile Mom and Dad were catching feisty bluegills about as fast as they could bait and cast. Then Rini got the hang of things, and there were three of us catching bluegills of that mysterious dimension, good-eating size. They fought like bluegills always do.

The fish bucket filled quickly. John, who was expected to clean the fish we'd eat for supper, decided to go ashore and get started. Rini and I rowed further down the bank, trying different spots.

Then I saw a darker shadow under the water just before the bobber went down. With admirable calm I said, "I believe I have a bass on."

I could give you the full Ernest Hemingway-Virgil Ward account of that piscine battle, but this is Upata Lake we're talking about. I boated my catch satisfactorily, held it up for my daughter to admire, then said, "Well, they aren't sensational eating, and they're not in season yet, and this guy is only hooked in the lip." I released the bass with a feeling of conscious virtue, having displayed my sportsmanship, my mastery of hook and line, my delicate taste buds, and my law-abiding nature, all at one go.

And when John came back down to the dock, Shireen gave him a vivid account of Mom's battle with Old Bucketmouth. (It's nice to have an eyewitness to one's nobler actions.) How big was this fish? As Shireen said when we drained our catch, "They always look bigger in the water."

But before then, I had said, "I know this isn't as fancy as cruising the Florida Inter-Coastal Waterway on a yacht—"

"Mom," she said, very seriously, "I love this; it brings back all sorts of pleasant memories of my childhood—"

"Hey, hey," I said, "I know, I was kidding. What do you want to do tomorrow? It's your last day."

"I don't have to leave till afternoon. Could we go fishing again in the morning?"

In Florida, I had eaten with daughter and friend at a classy sushi bar. Many kinds of elegant fish, mostly raw. We did not eat our sunfish raw. We ate them Minnesota style, deep-fried in beer batter, along with fresh asparagus and lambs' quarters and fresh-from-the-garden lettuce.

Next morning the big pumpkinseeds were biting. Rini caught the first two.

MORRISON COUNTY RECORD

Nature

Natural flavorings. Natural rights. Natural law.
Nature not nurture. Human nature. Naturally good—
If ever there was an idea that needed
to be written about leaf by leaf,
bird by bird, snake by snake,
this is it.

Just Part of the Family

May 24, 1989

The last of the hepaticas and the first blue violets and trilliums are blooming. The Juneberry tree is loaded with blossoms, and the perfume of wild plum flowers comes down the warm wind.

Half the beauty of spring is the promise of regeneration. To watch the grey sticks of winter veiling themselves in delicate green is to believe that everything can be healed, all things made new. It is hard to accept, walking through spring woods, that anything the human race does can inflict permanent damage on the fabric of life.

The damage did not start with modern humanity. The ancient world is full of once-thriving cities whose ruins are now buried in deserts—deserts that humans have produced by deforestation, overgrazing, bad agricultural practices. There are one-time harbors now miles inland, their anchorages long since buried in silt. There is an accelerating list of extinct organisms.

Of course, in the past, without the accuracy of today's science, we did not know what we were doing. And there were not so many of us.

We do not really want to believe that we are inflicting permanent and maybe irreparable harm on what we variously call Mother Nature, Mother Earth. We look at pictures from Prince

William Sound, reports on the Ozone Hole, well-documented instances of global warming, and then we look out at the woods, gloriously re-clothing the scars of winter in new green, and we say, "Well, gee. It can't be that bad."

There are solid economic reasons why some of us resist admitting that we can damage the web of life in permanent ways. If we own a company, run a company, even drive truck for a company, we want to believe that what we do is good. This is part paycheck loyalty, but it's also the awareness that we and our fellow workers are decent folks. Not the kind of people to give their mothers black eyes.

There are behavioral reasons, too. We are accustomed to living the way we're living. We may buy small, prepackaged changes (like the switch from records to tape cassettes or CDs) happily. But to consider that our whole lives may have to change— wow!—that's too much.

A teenager who treated his mother the way the human race treats the natural world would, at the very least, be in for some serious counseling. An adult who committed that sort of wholesale assault would probably wind up in jail.

The behavior and attitudes of human societies toward their planet are mostly like those of infants or toddlers. A nursing baby will sometimes bite not out of malice but because his gums hurt. He has no consciousness, till Mama lets him know about it, that he's inflicting pain. An angry two- or three-year-old may deeply and truly love his parents—hear him howl at separations!—but that doesn't always keep him from kicking or hitting.

Growing up is largely a matter of learning not to kick or hit, learning that Mom and Dad can be hurt. Learning, ultimately, that Mom and Dad are just infinite warehouses of warmth and nourishment and cuddles and fun and safety, but Mom and Dad are individuals with limitations, separate lives, needs of their own.

It is a traumatic experience the first time one looks at Mom or Dad and sees not a figure of god-like power but another human being, usually more or less the worse for wear from the strains of parenting.

In our relations with that bigger and older mother, we have stayed at the infant-toddler stage, in which we see no contradiction between "loving nature" and rearranging great hunks of it whenever that is to our immediate profit, advantage, or comfort.

Now, between the pressure of our own numbers, the immense powers we have developed—if not yet learned to control— and our advancing knowledge of how nature fits together, we are moving toward the point where we step away from the toddler stage in our relationship to our planet. Mother is not all-productive, all-healing, all-forgiving. We are not adored, only children but part of a large, complex family with some very strange siblings. We have to stop saying, "Gimme!" and "Me want!" and start saying, "Does this hurt?" and "Is there enough to go around?"

Paychecks aside, accustomed behaviors aside, we feel lonely and uncomfortable in this new relationship. Some of us are gritting our teeth in denial. Some of us are screaming and kicking Mom in the shins.

But we can make the transition. Most of us have already made it once (as children growing up) and helped others make it (as parents of children).

The third time can't be that hard.

LONG PRAIRIE LEADER

In Praise of Swamps

May 1, 1980

Nobody loves swamps. Swamps are too thick to swim, too thin to plow. Swamps breed mosquitoes and crawly creatures and trees that make lousy firewood. A drained swamp is a productive field. A filled swamp, especially near a lake, is saleable real estate. The only good swamp is a non-swamp.

Nobody loves swamps but water birds. Even a flooded field is a good overnight stopping ground for Canada geese on their way to the big swamps up north. A low field corner, a seasonal pothole, is heaven and haven to the small and not so small water birds, red-winged and yellow-headed blackbirds, night herons, woodcock, snipes. Swamps that hold water through the breeding season are natural hideaways for ducks. Even on big lakes, most birds like a shoreline to be more swamp than nice clean sand. Dry sand is comfortable for people in bathing suits to lie on, but silt and water and weedy places breed insects eaten by birds and frogs and fish eaten by bigger fish and people.

Nobody loves swamps but animals. Swamps are the natural home of the muskrat and beaver, the raccoon and mink and fisher. And the favorite browse of deer, red osier, grows best in low, damp places. The kind of forest people like—open and un-bushy, with nothing to snag the pants or wet the feet—is not really deer country at all. Even animals and birds who like drier habitats for their permanent lodgings find swamps splendid as hiding places. What's dry and level and accessible gets lumbered off, plowed up, platted out, converted to human uses. The boggy, no-account, too-wet-to-plow corners survive as wild places. Every biologist I've ever consulted says the same thing: what kills off grouse and pheasants isn't hunters or bad weather or predators like the fox. It's lack of habitat. Lack of shelter. Swamps, boggy old, buggy old swamps, are shelter.

Nobody loves swamps but flood fighters and people concerned with erosion control. A swamp is a sponge, a filter, a brake. Water soaks into a swamp and stays there, and, when the swamp is saturated, the water that runs off runs clear, not silted, slowly. The fewer swamps and swales and boggy places there are in a given watershed, the more severe the flood problems will be. Building dams and levees and straightening out rivers only lets the water go faster, ripping along with all the topsoil it can pick up—good fertile farmland—that in due time will silt up the artificial lakes, turn the southern reaches of rivers into soup and enlarge the deltas in the Gulf of Mexico.

But building dams and levees is dramatic, heroic-looking; it eases our human urge to be masters of our fate. It puts people to work, too. Chambers of commerce and politicians running for office love dams and levees and flood-control projects. They make a community look progressive. The mayor or congressman or senator can get his picture in the paper, his name attached to the project, this concrete contribution to the well-being of his constituents. X million tax dollars come back from Washington to the district.

Leaving swamps undrained is much cheaper and, in the long run, better for the landscape, better for what ecologists call the biome—the total community of creatures sharing that watershed. Mosquitoes and dragonflies, swallows and marshhawks, otters and deer, cornfields upstream and living rooms down—all are better off with the proper proportion of swamps just left alone. Unfortunately it's hard for people to leave things alone. It isn't dramatic. People can't debate it and vote on it and get their names attached to it. The best they can do is get an injunction, and then they'll be described as standing in the way of progress. Protecting a swamp? You've got to be kidding.

Nobody loves swamps but biologists and eccentrics and now and then a poet. Henry Thoreau, who wrote *Walden*, said once, "In wildness is the salvation of the world." He took his friend Nathanial Hawthorne, who wrote *The Scarlet Letter* and thought a lot about original sin, into his favorite swamp one day. Before Thoreau could possibly point out any of the beautiful and beautifully-adapted wild things that only live in swamps, Hawthorne said, "Let us get out of this dreadful hole."

We are told in Genesis that Adam and Eve were put by God in a garden "eastward in Eden" and that "a river went out of Eden to water the garden." We are not told whether the river ran through any swamps.

LONG PRAIRIE LEADER

Round the Bend

August 28, 1980

There are people who vacation by driving all day, people who fly to Vegas and lose all their money, and people who go to Europe and "do" ten countries in fourteen days. Then there are people who get where they are going by muscle power, and, when they are there, they sleep on the ground.

Last week John and I loaded up a box of food, a tent and sleeping bags, some rain and shine gear, and Old Blue, the fiberglass canoe Eric bought with some of the money from his sow's first litter of pigs. After a two-hour drive, we were paddling down the Shell River.

There is something magical about canoeing. A carried canoe is heavy and clumsy; a canoe in water glides like movement in a dream. One stroke with the paddle, and it just goes. On a river, it really doesn't even need a paddle stroke. The water takes it.

The Shell River was named for the big clams that live in it. At one time a pearl button factory existed at Shell City. We had no trouble seeing clams, shells, stones, eelgrass, duckweed, and fish through the water of the Shell River or the Crow Wing, into which the Shell runs. The water is what sporting magazines always refer to as "gin-clear," perhaps suggesting that there is something intoxicating about boating on that kind of water.

The intoxication is there, all right. But it seems odd to make a comparison between clean running water and man-distilled spirits, as if this comparison is flattering to the natural product. The water of the Shell and the Crow Wing is the color of water first out of the sky. The color of water without oil or chemicals or silt. The color of water. Not gin-clear. Water clear.

A lot of our paddling carried us through the Huntersville State Forest. Some of it was oak woods, some of it pine. There were little sandy bars where sandpipers tipped and great blue herons stood exactly like dead tree branches till they lifted their big slow wings and flapped off down the river. When we were close enough, we could hear the sound of feathers rowing air: whoosh, whoosh, whoosh. There were a lot of ducks, too—mallards and teal—in groups mostly, enough out of molt to fly short distances but not wanting to fly far yet. They would lift up in front of us and fly down to the next bend. When we got close to them they would take off again.

There were plenty of signs of beaver activity (we saw a couple of big lodges) and even more of muskrats at work. Once a young muskrat swam so close to the side of the boat that I could have touched him with the paddle. I could see his sleek-furred body, his whiskers, his feet paddling along like a dog's except that they were submerged, the double stream of air bubbles running back from his nose. He didn't bother me, and I don't think I bothered him.

We hauled out once at a grassy place to stretch our legs and again under the old Huntersville Bridge to get something cold to drink from the Huntersville Store. There we saw the only mess of the whole trip: a pile of pop and beer cans and plastic garbage bags piled up under the bridge. There is no camp here, only the Huntersville Store. No automobile traffic comes here; the old Huntersville Bridge is condemned, and automobile traffic moves across the new bridge further up. Only canoeists come here, and they come only to patronize the Huntersville Store. If there were only a few cans, canoeists might take them away when they go. But once a garbage pile gets to a certain ungainly size, nobody is going to clear it off voluntarily. If the proprietor of the Huntersville Store would put out a garbage can and empty it from time to time, people would probably use it. But he can't see the garbage from his store. So the garbage keeps piling up.

About three in the afternoon we pulled out at Big Bend Camp. There were only two other canoeists there. We put up the tent, napped, woke and cooked the small walleye and big perch John had caught coming down, along with a steak and some vegetables from the garden; then we paddled back up river a ways for some evening fishing. All afternoon we had seen fish—sucker and wall-eye and northern—lying in the deep pools of the river, all with their heads pointing upstream, waiting for food to float into their mouths. We cast, we changed lures, we tried bobber-fishing with night crawlers and leeches. We came home empty-handed, but that didn't seem important. In the near dark we sat by the fire, talking a little and then not talking. I sang a song I learned when I was ten:

> If there were witchcraft, I'd make two wishes;
> A winding road that beckons me to roam;
> Then I would wish for a blazing campfire,
> To welcome me when I'm returning home.

The Girl Scout leader who taught me that song, a silver-haired little Scotswoman named Josephine Pinckney, was old when I knew her first and must be long dead. The sister with whom I sang it is dead, too.

> But in this real world there is no witchcraft,
> And golden wishes do not grow on trees.
> Our fondest daydreams must be the magic
> To welcome back these golden memories.

We washed in the privacy of darkness, air and water temperatures the same, streaky moonlight through the woods. Whippoorwills called; I'd never heard them before. We crawled into the familiar smells and textures—tent and sleeping bag and woods dark. Tomorrow there would be more to paddle, rapids to run, new birds round the bend.

LONG PRAIRIE LEADER

Waiting for Sunnies

June 30, 1982

In most years, by the middle of June we are spending a couple of hours a day dunking earthworms with a light bobber and hauling substantial messes of golden pumpkinseeds and speckled bluegills. Not this year, not yet. We sit and we soak the worms and we look at the sky and we move to a new location and we soak some more worms. So far no action.

But we know that when the action comes, it will be good. I think it was Louis Bromfield who observed that, ounce for ounce, sunfish are as aggressive as any fish in the world and that, if anybody ever succeeds in breeding a five-pound bluegill, fishermen will have a fish that will compete with the smallmouth bass or the muskellunge or tarpon as a sport fish. And fortunately we do not have to travel to the ends of the earth for good sunfishing. Sunfish are feisty, tasty, pretty, common, and prolific. And this time of the year, as regular as robins' eggs or the first wild roses, the small, aggressive males and the big, bulging females spawn in the shallows of Big Swan Lake. Except not this year, not yet. We're still soaking worms and waiting, this year.

Of course there are things to be said for just sitting in a boat. Some of the best conversations I've had have been in boats while waiting for the fish to bite. They have been largely silent conversations, but that doesn't hurt. If we sit across a living room or a table from somebody, there's an unwritten law that we have to talk; however, no such law applies while fishing. In fact too much noise can scare off the fish. So there is no pressure to be smart or witty or profound in a fishing boat. It's very nice sometimes to have conversations limited to, "Any bumps?" or "Nice one!"

Because in a fishing boat we are sitting and waiting for something to happen, I notice things I wouldn't notice at another time: cloud shapes, the numerous varieties of insects and birds that hang out around lakes, wave motion, and colors in the water. A few nights ago we had a slight wind, just enough to make little choppy ripples. The lake water was medium blue under a clear, near-sunset sky. I realized that each little wavelet showed under its peak a flash of deeper blue like the eye in a peacock's tail feather. A couple of nights later we had similar wind conditions, but occasionally the sky was thinly overcast. This time the lake water showed almost gunmetal grey with flashes of green reflected from the green leaves of the shoreline. At other times I've seen wave colors of blue and gold, blue and silver, blue and rose.

Water in itself is a magical medium. It is not surprising that so many mythologies contain both lovely water beings—mermaids, nixes, undines, silkies—and scary water monsters. There is a haunting Scots ballad about a silkie—"I am a man upon the land, I am a silkie on the sea"—and the mortal woman he loves and the half-human child she bears him. When the child is old enough to go with its father into deep water, the silkie comes to claim it and tells his lover: "And you will marry a gunner good. And a right fine gunner I'm sure he'll be. And the very first shot that e'er he fires, Will kill both my young son and me."

I can understand how stories like that came about as I look at the strange underwater world of stone, sand, gravel, reeds, coon tails, and diaphanous castles of moss. I also can understand, why water is so important symbolically in so many religions—holy water, baptismal water, water of life, and the water of change and cleansing.

Sounds that might be harsh or ordinary on land take on a special quality over water—the barking of dogs, for instance, or the distant roaring of cars or tractors, and, of course, bird songs and cries. I still remember the first time I heard a loon scream in the middle of the night. I was nine-tenths asleep in a lake cabin after a trip from California, and I didn't realize it was a bird; I thought it was a woman screaming in terror. It scared the liver out of me. But a loon call across the lake when I too am on the water is haunting and lovely.

We've had some extraordinary encounters with birds and animals while waiting for fish to bite. We have watched mother ducks swimming with their young, and once or twice we have seen coots do their running-on-the-water mating dance. One time we were plagued by a lot of tiny, hungry perch that kept suicidally swallowing up the bait meant for bigger fish. As we tossed the perch into the water we attracted a great blue heron who would swoop down to catch up our discards. To have a bird that large, that majestic following us around like a dog looking for scraps is a strange feeling.

Strangest and most magical of all was the morning we were on Sawbill Lake up on the edge of the Boundary Waters Canoe Area, fishing unproductively in a fog. I don't remember which of us noticed first the round rock that seemed to move. There was one dark, sleek head in the water . . . then another, then another, and yet another. We were being examined by a bunch of otters, very probably a family of mother and three young. They swam around us, slipping in and out of the clear grey water, looking at us curiously with their catlike, intelligent faces and from time to time making a noise that was halfway between a sneeze and a window shade rolling up suddenly. I don't know how long the otters' visit lasted—five minutes, perhaps ten. Then they were off about their business. I'll remember it all my life.

A person can do worse than soak a few worms and wait for the fishing to improve.

LONG PRAIRIE LEADER

Talking with Animals

January 12, 1992

In these cold blue mornings, Sam comes in hungrily for water and a bit of kidney and a chance to rub on human ankles.

Sam really does not need either the nourishment or the warmth. Her striped tabby coat (tiger grey on her back, tinged with red on her belly) is dense, and, though the tips of the fur are cold against a stroking hand, the cat in the fur is well-muffled and comfortable. She has an insulated cubbyhole up in the garage, a steady supply of dry cat food, plus all the wild creatures she can catch.

Unlike most domestic animals, Sam could probably get along fine without the Rylanders to care for her. But I think she enjoys our company. Certainly when she comes in these cold mornings, she gives us lengthy meowed conversations about the wind conditions and the temperature of the snow. We talk back to her, of course.

Most people who have animals wind up talking to them. This is true even of the animals that live in barns and sheds. Some animals, of course, are more responsive than others. Over the years we have kept and raised dogs, pigs, steers, sheep, and chickens, and we have probably talked to them in about that order.

Sometimes the animals, like Sam or a happy dog, clearly enjoy the conversational interchange with people. Old readers of this column will remember discussions of Miss Piggy, our son Eric's brood sow. She joined the domestic arrangements while quite young, and, as a full-grown, well over 600-pound sow, she still loved to be talked to and have her ears scratched. She held up her end of the conversation with grunts and wiggles.

Most domestic animals will come charging up to the fence if you have food for them, but it's always difficult to tell if they are coming for you or the food. I don't know, when a ewe was in hard labor, whether my voice was soothing to her or not. But it seemed natural for me, back when I was doing sheep obstetrics, to say things like, "okay, now," and "steady, girl," as the little woolies came into the world of the Rylander barn.

Humans have one kind of relationship with pets, animals who share their affections and often their homes. They have a rather different kind of relationship with the animals they keep as a source of food or income.

It used to be that almost everybody, if they didn't have a horse in the back yard or chickens in the barn, at least knew somebody who did. This kind of relationship between humans and animals is becoming rarer and rarer. Perhaps as a result, there are increasing numbers of people for whom the keeping of animals to eat or sell is a form of slavery with overtones of cannibalism.

I have a certain respect for conscientious vegetarians. (I have rather less respect for the squeamish people who say, "Oooo, how can you kill an animal?" but will happily eat meat that somebody else has killed.) I think, however, that the sort of vegetarian who advocates the total abandonment of animal food hasn't thought the problem through.

Most domestic animals—cattle, sheep, hogs—are either incapable of living in the wild or (like the feral razorback hogs of the South) become destroyers of native wildlife if they are turned loose. If humans give up bacon and beefsteak, what will happen to all the breeds of animals, developed over the generations, that exist wholly to feed their human breeders?

It's unpleasant to realize that we all live by eating other beings. (It's true that vegetables don't try to escape or scream aloud, but they certainly are living organisms.) But in fact we do, all of us—even vegetarians whose diets are sustained by a bug and weed-killing agriculture.

Unfortunately, the traditional relationship between shepherd and sheep, stock and herder is becoming harder to sustain for reasons that have nothing to do with animal liberationism. More and more, farmers are pressed into production techniques in which their animals are regarded as meat and milk machines. You still see farm auctions where the cows are named, but the days of Flossie and Bossie, Miss Piggy and the Little Red Hen are numbered, not because of human selfishness and cruelty but because of the whole "get big or get out" disease that afflicts agriculture in the United States.

Most farmers don't like this. Livestock raisers are often in hog or dairy production because they like the animals with which they work, and they will tell you so. Treating animals and soil and people as machines is bad for animals and soil and people, but it is easier to denounce animal exploitation than to devise an economics and a politics that would encourage farmers to farm not just sustainably but kindly.

Sam finishes her snack and her visit, crawls under the stove for a while, then asks to be let out and trots off across the snowy world, tail up. If the human race vanished today, Sam and her fellows would continue to catch mice in the ruins. Her relationship with us is easy on both species.

Other relationships between humans and animals are more complicated. And of course the relationships between humans and humans are the most complicated of all.

MORRISON COUNTY RECORD

Stray Cats

October 11, 1982

I had gone out to the kennel to feed the puppies when I heard the strange, sharp sound coming from behind the haystack. We have plenty of animal noises around here at all times—dogs, chickens, sheep, cattle, Millie the duck, two guinea fowl, plus birds and squirrels. But this was unfamiliar: it was a kitten.

Though I grew up with cats and am fond of them, we don't own a cat. Kelly, the terrier who thinks she's a human, would never forgive us if we introduced a cat into the house. She is jealous of our association with the kenneled springers.

There are cats around, though. They are wild cats, and I don't mean mountain lions or lynxes. They are cats gone wild—the unwanted offspring of house or barn cats—who have wandered off or maybe been dumped out in the country by somebody who didn't want to make or find a home for them or go through the trauma of knocking them on the head. "They'll find a home catching mice in somebody's barn," I can imagine the kitten-dumper saying to himself just before he drives away.

Most such animals do not live long. They are the cats whose broken bodies you see along the road. Or they starve. But those who do survive multiply quickly and become entirely wild—they don't want to be petted and fed saucers of milk. So it didn't seem impossible that there might be kittens around.

Following my ears, I located the crying one. The black plastic cover on the stack of hay bales was looped up at one point, making a pocket in which rain water had accumulated. When I climbed up onto the stack, I discovered a kitten, head just barely above water, small legs slashing frantically, about to drown in eight inches of stagnant water on the backside of the haystack.

I lifted it out, holding it at arm's length. Covered with green algae scum, it was wet, wretched, exhausted, and stinking to high heaven. Its eyes were open—bright blue—and the fur under the slime was black and white. In the moments when it wasn't crying I heard less urgent cries. Lifting up the stack cover, I discovered two more kittens, another black-and-white one and an all-black one. They were up in a recess among the hay bales.

Of course, they were adorable. So strong is my maternal instinct that even baby alligators would probably drawn an "aww" reaction from me, and, as I said, I grew up with cats. But I also knew that even one wild cat around the place, catching birds and menacing small chickens, was a nuisance. Wild domestic cats are not part of the natural ecology of central Minnesota. They are like Dutch elm disease or toxic waste, an accidental and destructive glitch in the natural order. If these kittens grew up, the nuisance would be quadrupled.

Nevertheless, I put the green, wet, stinky kitten back with its littermates.

Next day I couldn't resist taking a peep to see if the wet one had survived the cold fall night. The kitten was as sleek as the others. Mama must have come back and bathed it. I also discovered that there were four kittens, not three. Another black-and-white-spotted one must have been back further among the bales.

By the next day all the kittens were out of the stack and prowling around on the ground, climbing clumsily but with determination, mewing. Their bellies were still round with milk. Mama had visited them again.

By the following morning they were crawling all over a fifty-foot radius. Two of them were scrambling around on the hay bales. Their little tails stuck up like exclamation points.

As the morning passed, their cries became louder, and their activity level slackened. Their bellies were flat. By afternoon, a couple were hardly moving. It was clear that Mama had not been back the night before. They could not live much longer without human intervention.

Well, maybe we could find homes for four kittens. I mixed

up some leftover lamb milk replacer and found an eyedropper. They were too small for a baby bottle and far too young to do anything with a saucer of milk except sneeze.

One of them I hardly expected to live. It was limp and silent, making no movements but an occasional convulsive retraction of the head. Its pink mouth was cold inside, which I knew was a bad sign from trying to save chilled lambs, weakling pigs, puppies who didn't get a tit soon enough. But I managed to get some milk down the throat of Weakest, what didn't dribble out the corners of the mouth or bubble up out the nose. Another kitten was slightly stronger—Weaker, not Weakest—able to mew faintly and swallow weakly. The black kitten, whom I found myself thinking of as Darth, climbed all over me. The black-and-white kitten I had rescued from a watery grave was pretty strong too.

I left them outside after their rations, hoping the mother would return. But it was cold. Eric brought them into the house. I fed them again around supper time. This time even Weakest was mewing a little and trying to suck. They were evacuating, which I figured was a good sign. But they couldn't clean themselves of cat mess or spilled milk, and their mother wasn't here to do it. I wiped them off with a warm damp cloth.

A couple of hours later, Weakest was dead in the box. Weaker and my little sailor, Jonah, were mewing and scrambling and gulping down milk. So was Darth, but not as vigorously as before. I wondered where their mother had come from, if she had been killed, how many litters of unwanted kittens she had born, how many these might bear if they lived. I thought of pictures I'd seen that day on the news, of human refugees in the wrong place at the wrong time, now dead. I was glad they were not my children, but they were somebody's children. I lifted Weakest, a rumpled, dirty bundle of small bones, cooling fur, out of the box.

At four in the morning kitten cries woke me, and I came down with eyedropper and milk. There was another little corpse—Weaker—to take out. Both Darth and Jonah were limper, less strong. Darth wasn't walking anymore. Twenty-four hours before he had been scrambling up hay bales and making practice runs. I could see him as an adult cat, black with a watered-silk stripe pattern and a fine piratical swagger. I coaxed a little more milk into him.

At seven he was dead, his stomach still round from my last feeding. Maybe the milk was too weak, or too strong. Maybe they just couldn't make it without their mother.

Jonah lasted through one more feeding. At one-thirty that

afternoon I laid him by the back door. There is something about death that shrinks animals. There he was, a rumpled, filthy bundle I could almost have hidden in my fist.

Eric had buried the others, but he was busy with chores, and I was canning. Jonah lay there till almost dark. I buried him where the soil was soft, under the compost heap, cool earth sifting into soft, dirty fur.

MORRISON COUNTY RECORD

Death in the Woods

October 14, 1987

I can't walk through these lovely fall woods, mushroom-picking sack in hand, without thinking about death.

Mind you, I am not one of those hypersensitive folks who watches the weather reports on television and greets the cool air and occasional fall rain with such moans and cries and snivels that one would think the end of the world was at hand. Those folks all look healthy enough, yet hearing them go on about the end of summer, they might as well be orchids that shrivel with the slightest touch of cool air or relatives of the Wicked Witch of the West, who melted like brown sugar in the presence of water.

And despite all those melancholy poems about falling leaves, I cannot manage to summon up so much as a premonitory shiver when I watch the leaves fall. Here is this little package of plant cells that has done a yoeman job all summer, converting sunlight into sugar to nourish its tree. Now corky cells block its stem; its supply of chlorophyll cut off, it flares with the golds of carotene and the reds of xanthine. I never look at a woods full of turned (i.e., dying) leaves without thinking: What a way to go!

One day the leaf breaks loose, whirls down in a graceful spiral, lies underfoot a day or two—a brilliant calling card of frost, crunching deliciously under the feet of passers-by.

Then as the insects and the bacteria and the saprophytic plants get to it, the leaf dwindles to a skeleton, a whisper of ghost cells on the way to becoming the blackest, richest soil in the world. Come warm weather, roots will enter it, seeds will germinate in it, its energies will rise again to the sun.

Even the fall of a whole tree, the crash that takes down fifty or a hundred or three hundred years of living, is no catastrophe so long as the tree is part of a healthy, self-renewing forest. The engine that makes self-renewal possible is death, picking off the leaf that will serve no purpose in winter, pruning out the old trees and letting sunlight in to the forest floor. Death, followed by decay.

It is my observation that people who are in the physical state of the turned leaf or the hollow tree often are ready to let go, to give their lives back willingly to what made them. But it is hard for the living to let go of the dying, not only because it will hurt to have them gone but because, when the last tree of the old generation goes, we stand on the skyline alone. And miraculous machinery, designed mostly to help in the acute crises of accident, has made it possible to keep the dying in a twilight state for years. When the will and desire to keep on have faded, when brain and bowels and skin and digestive tract and heart and lungs must all be kept going through constant intervention, dying is not a natural change but strenuous, painful, and undignified, a profoundly unnatural exercise in futility.

The kindest thing we can do for the people we love is grant them what fall gives the leaf—the chance to die with a little grace, a little flare.

If we don't like to talk about death, we don't like even to think about decay. Wherever the energies of the dear departed have gone, they do not linger in the body, unless we are thinking in terms of chemicals and atoms. But when "ashes to ashes" is spoken, it is often over a loved one, embalmed and coffined and vaulted in a way to make the transition to dust as slow as possible. We dress and paint them up as if we expect the Last Trump to summon our dead to an audition as TV weathercasters.

In spring, the dead of past seasons are resurrected in sprout and leaf and flower. In fall it is decay that blooms. The transition of raw stump and fallen trunk to black life-making earth goes on in a riot of molds and mosses and mushrooms, each species performing its specialized tasks of breaking down old cells and remaking them, then shedding spores and melting away into the forest floor. And as the grown, live trees support whole communities of birds and mammals and insects, so the stumps and logs support their own communities of varied life. This time of year the oyster and honey mushrooms nourish other lives all the way from the bottom of the food chain (each one has its own particular kind of insect lodger) to the top—me with my mushroom bag.

As the Preacher said a long time ago: to everything there is a season.

LONG PRAIRIE LEADER

The Flags of Acertilia

October 1, 1989

The flags of Acertilia are flying.

I am, not by birth but by the heart's adoption and life's process of naturalization, a citizen of that country. Born in the central valley of California, raised in a dying town in the Nevada desert and the burgeoning suburbs of coastal California, married into the fringes of Academe and the frayed edges of Bohemia, I came to the blue lakes and glacier-mounded hills of Acertilia as an adult.

I didn't know I was an Acertilian till this spring. Then I saw a map of Minnesota, which lists not towns and highways but biological communities. Prairie. Pine forest. River-bottom. Angled up the map, from its southeast corner to just a little beyond where I live in Todd County, is a long spur of mixed deciduous hardwood forest—or country once mixed deciduous hardwood forest. When pastures are unmowed and fields lie fallow, the earth of that country still works its way back to mixed deciduous hardwood forest.

Each biological community on that map is identified by its dominant plant species, written in scientific Latin. The dominant species of these woods are the maples (*Acer*) and the basswoods (*Tilia*). The place where I feel most at home, the place of my best poems and deepest loyalties, is given on that map its proper name. Acertilia.

Acertilianism, like any other form of patriotism, begins as a matter not only of the heart but of the senses. My father, a westerner and a pilot, used to say he always felt he was coming home when he hit the western downslope of the Rockies. There are people who are hooked on the smell of salt water, the whiff of rabbit brush, the resin of pine, even the tang of pickles in certain neighborhood delis. Right now, as the banners of Acertilia flash their seasonal changes, the smells of home are damp and wild and mushroomy enough to wake the dead.

One of the nice things about being an Acertilian is that Acertilianism has very little historical baggage. There are no Acertilian political parties. There are no Acertilian heroes. Nobody has ever been challenged in the political arena because he was insufficiently Acertilian. There has never been an Acertilian loyalty oath. Nobody has ever been blacklisted or purged for anti-Acertilianism.

Even old Acertilians are not offended if you burn the red and gold banners of that nation. I drink the blossoms of those trees in tea, eat their blood (boiled) on pancakes and burn their fibrous flesh all winter long. So long as the logging is done with care, Acertilia is in no way diminished.

Wars, or at least battles, have been fought in and over parts of Acertilia—Dakota against Anishinabe, red men against white men, railroads and banks and farmers and homeowners against and among each other—but Acertilia cannot, properly speaking, be defended by force of arms. War is even harder on forests than bulldozers. Good husbandry alone can defend Acertilia, along with decent, modest living—living which admits that humans are part of the world's biotic community but not the purpose of that community, not the planetary Great Panjandrum to which all things living owe tribute.

One of the things we who are Great Panjandrums do is to generalize, to abstract. If we did not, there would be no identifying of tree species, and we could not talk about Acertilia, or much less. Abstraction allows us to get beyond the flair of the nostrils at the scent of familiar trees, allows us to make poems, laws, deed descriptions, environmental impact statements.

Abstraction also allows us to cut our religious and political ideas free from their grounding in the particular. We can preach about God's love while walking past the homeless. We can demand laws to prevent flag burning, because we love our country, while incinerating the flesh of that country, her oil and coal and air and water and possible future, in the interests of comfort and the fast buck. We can defend ourselves, or plan to defend ourselves, with weapons that, if used, would leave the surviving cockroaches cackling with laughter over phrases like "fruited plain" and "land of opportunity."

Acertilians are primitive and stupid and proud of it. They know their country is not transportable. They know that, though tough, it is eminently destroyable. They love their country as a woman loves her husband or her child. Not the picture. Not the concept. Not the word "marriage" or "motherhood." But the near, the particular, the specific, the tangible, the Now. The skin responding to the kiss. The blackbirds and grackles yakking brassily as they gather to go south. The seasonal flags of the heart's country, which fall and rot and bud and eat sun and color and fall again.

ST. CLOUD TIMES

The Tail over the Berm Door

June 9, 1991

Our earth-sheltered house has an ordinary sort of front door and a back door that tunnels into the earthern berm like the entrance to the dwarfs' mine in "Snow White." I had been hanging up clothes on the lines just outside the back door. When I turned to go back into the house, the tail of a large garter snake hung lazily down over the door.

Quite a few snakes live in our berm, and that's fine with us. We're neither of us snake-phobic, and we're conscious that there are no poisonous snakes in central Minnesota. The snakes probably keep the mouse population around the house down some.

This big fellow was basking in the morning warmth. The rest of him was concealed in the grass and stones, but, like a very small child playing peek-a-boo, he may have thought that if he couldn't see us, we couldn't see him. His tail was hanging down like a rope or a handle.

I couldn't resist. I grabbed it. The snake reacted much as you or I. For a moment he was absolutely still ("What's this?" I could imagine him thinking), and then he was pulling and thrashing. I let him go.

That afternoon, as I was cutting up onions for spaghetti, John pointed out the window. Two deer stood in the edge of the woods, just where our front yard begins. They were not more than fifty feet from the house.

We knew deer abounded in the woods, at least in the summer. There were deer trails everywhere, and we had seen their sharp prints in our garden often enough. But we didn't actually see deer very often.

Perhaps these deer were too young to be very timid. They were probably yearlings whose mothers had chased them away when they had this year's fawns. We stood and watched for ten or fifteen minutes as they browsed on fresh young twigs, their elegant, slender, red coats shining with health and spring. There is a magic in being that close to a wild creature. I had felt it when I held the snake in my hands.

Eventually John, who wanted to haul one more load of garden mulch before dinner, slipped out the back door. I thought certainly that the sound of the door shutting, then the pickup starting, would drive those deer right out of the yard—but no. When the truck left, they looked up and pricked their ears, then went back to browsing. One lay down for a while, right next to my flowerbed. After a time she came even further into the yard. She was eating dandelions.

The deer visited at least half an hour. I don't know exactly when they left because I had gone back to my spaghetti sauce.

Two days ago, I was transplanting flowers and herbs into a new herb bed I was making. I had been dipping water out of one of our rain barrels. This time when I bent over, I saw a young ribbon snake, the green and white stripey kind, swimming around in the water and trying to get up the slick plastic side of the barrel and failing. I reached in and lifted him out and put him up safely onto the berm.

This morning we had a nice thundershower. I set a board across the rain barrel and put a clean plastic bucket on the board to catch the rainwater with which I like to rinse my hair. When I went to take my bucket away, either the same ribbon snake or his sibling swam around in the barrel. Pretty tired he looked, too.

This time when I lifted him out, I took him into the kitchen so John could admire his slick, striped body and red, forked tongue. If the little snake had been tired in the barrel, being lifted out had given him new vigor. He writhed around in my hand, making "s" curves, trying to look menacing. Eventually he struck the base of my thumb. He was too small for his tiny mouth to even pinch, and his fangs couldn't break my skin, but he was going through all the motions of the terrible venomous serpent. A snake who doesn't know who his friends are.

I put him up on the berm a good distance from the rain barrel. "Don't fall into the rain barrel again, silly serpent," I told him. I'm still trying to figure out how he managed that—not once but twice.

Sometimes I have to go after subjects to write about. Sometimes they walk into my yard or fall into my rain barrel or hang their tails down over the berm door.

MORRISON COUNTY RECORD